Happy BIRTHDAY CLARKE,

Love the history!
Love the game!

Jim Calder

Lacrosse
The Ancient Game

Lacrosse
The Ancient Game

WRITTEN BY | ILLUSTRATED BY

JIM CALDER & RON FLETCHER | DAVID CRAIG & ARNOLD JACOBS

ORAL TRADITION BY

✦ DELMOR JACOBS ✦

ANCIENT GAME PRESS ™

Published in 2011 by Ancient Game Press

Photo reproduction of David Craig's artwork by ICON PHOTOGRAPHY

For order inquiries you can reach us at:
   Lacrosse: The Ancient Game
   Unit 106
   3007 Kingston Road
   Toronto, ON, Canada
   M1M 1P1

or email us at:
   info@lacrossetheancientgame.com

Library and Archives Canada Cataloguing in Publication

Calder, Jim
   Lacrosse : the ancient game / written by Jim Calder & Ron Fletcher ;
   illustrated by David Craig & Arnold Jacobs ; oral tradition by Delmor Jacobs.

Includes bibliographical references.
ISBN 978-0-9869314-0-6 (bound). — ISBN 978-0-9869314-1-3 (pbk.)

1. Lacrosse — Canada — History. 2. Lacrosse — United States — History.
3. Indians of North America — Games. I. Fletcher, Ron II. Craig, David
III. Jacobs, Arnold IV. Jacobs, Delmor V. Title.

GV989.C24 2011   796.34'70971   C2011-905115-X

Design by Gillian Stead

Printed in China

Contents

To all those in the lacrosse family
who love this game like no other

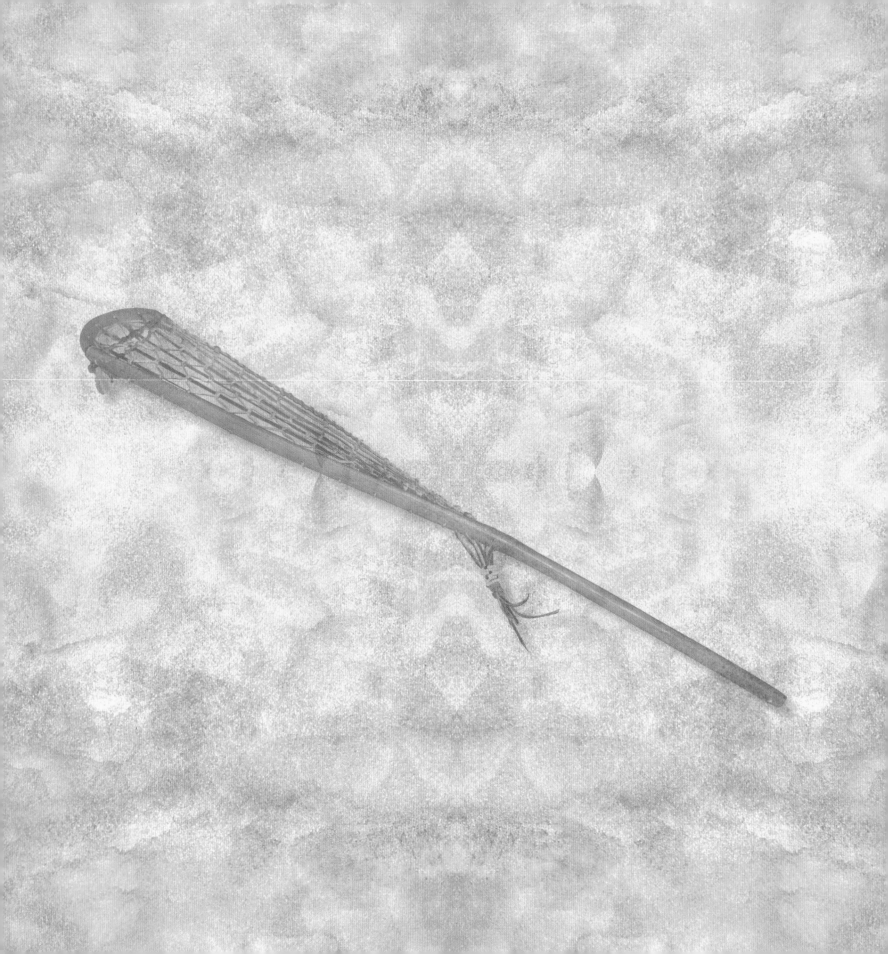

Foreword

Gary Gait
WOMEN'S LACROSSE COACH
SYRACUSE UNIVERSITY

This book, *Lacrosse — The Ancient Game,* brings to life through vivid literary and artistic means the tradition and history of the game of lacrosse. The game is presented from two sides — that of ritual and healing as well as that of competition.

Readers of this book will learn about the game's growth and expansion from an exclusively Native American tradition to a truly international sport. Readers will also become familiar with the historical events, places and people who shaped the tradition into what we now know as "lacrosse."

From an historical standpoint, the artwork in this book illuminates what the game meant to the Native Americans. It was much more than just a game: it was something that brought people together; it was spiritual and healing.

While the rules, techniques, equipment and intent of the game have changed significantly since it moved beyond Native American culture, what remains the same at the core of the game — and what makes lacrosse so great — is the exhibition of speed, skill and intelligence demonstrated by the players on the field.

This book is a must-have for the true lacrosse enthusiast who wants to understand the history of the game and its incredible origins.

Gary Gait

Ball Play, George Catlin (1796–1872). Lithograph with applied watercolor, 1875–1878.
Amon Carter Museum of American Art, Fort Worth, Texas

Preface

The region now considered "the Cradle of Lacrosse" extends inland from Lake Ontario and the lower St. Lawrence River on both sides of the U.S.–Canada border: north into Ontario and Quebec, and south into upstate New York and the Finger Lakes district.

For over a millennium, the game has played a significant role in the cultural, spiritual and recreational lives of the region's First Nations people. Historical evidence of similar "stickball" games has been found throughout the Americas. These games were invented and played by vibrant indigenous cultures that thrived well before European contact. "Two-stick" versions played by the Seminole and Choctaw were gloriously captured in the nineteenth-century paintings of George Catlin and Charles Deas.

As with many aboriginal rituals, there are yin and yang qualities to lacrosse. It was considered a "little brother to war," providing its participants an opportunity to develop their physical fitness and toughness in preparation for battle, but also, perhaps more importantly, it served as a form of "medicine." The game was used in communication with the Creator to heal those who suffered from illness and to settle disputes between neighboring tribes. In the Native tradition, the game *was* and *is* played for the enjoyment of the Creator. Winning and losing are secondary to playing the game.

The First Nations people of upstate New York, Quebec and Ontario eventually introduced the sport to early European settlers, who enthusiastically embraced the game. Their descendants and later immigrants would further shape the game through standardized rules and technological innovations. They would also launch the earliest university and club teams.

This book, *Lacrosse — The Ancient Game*, adds to the sport's existing literature by exploring the game's vibrant cultural and historical roots. In the last forty years, the game has seen incredible growth, with the introduction of the plastic stick, the successful operation of professional teams, expansion of the game at the university, high school and local levels, and the accelerated push towards Olympic-level international competition.

As lacrosse aficionados, we love the growth that the game is currently enjoying. It is a special game — unique in the world — really the only existing team sport that is spiritual in nature. You feel that magical difference almost immediately when you pick up a stick for the first time.

In response to this growth, it is important that we respect the game and acknowledge the traits that make it special. This respect comes through knowing its history and culture. Once we understand that we are part of this remarkable history, we may develop a passion and love for the game that allows us to take it to a higher level.

Lacrosse — The Ancient Game can be seen as a "gateway" book, perhaps leading the reader to investigate the handful of detailed academic and anthropological history books published on the sport, perhaps even inspiring future research and writing.

I believe lacrosse history can be divided into three eras. This book covers the first era, which ends in 1883 with George Beers' final visit to Europe. The second era ends in 1970 and includes the growth of university lacrosse and the first professional leagues. The modern era begins in 1971 with the invention of the plastic stick, national television coverage, major university and professional league events, the growth of international lacrosse, and the use of media to create star players.

The book begins with the telling of the oral tradition by Faithkeeper Dao Jao Dre (Delmor Jacobs) of the Cayuga Nation in the Iroquois Confederacy. Dao Jao Dre explains the significance of "the Creator's game" within the traditional culture of the Cayuga from his unique perspective as a Faithkeeper.

The Creator's game appears early in the creation stories of Dao Jao Dre's people and plays an integral part in the holistic view of their time on the planet. It is important to know how the game fits into the overall story of his people so that we can understand the essence of our game. All lacrosse players share a sense of the special nature of our sport, though we may not quite be able to put it into words. Dao Jao Dre tells us just what this special nature is and why it is so strong.

The book also features some of the seminal moments in the history of lacrosse, passed down to us through diaries, journals, books and paintings. It takes the reader on a 300-year

Sioux Playing Ball. Painting by Charles Deas. Courtesy Gilcrease Museum, Tulsa, Oklahoma

journey from the earliest written observations of the Native sport to the 1880s and the production of "Flannery Celebrated Lacrosse Sticks."

In 2017, the world of lacrosse will celebrate the 150th anniversary of George Beers' standardized instructions on how to play the game — the first set of formal rules as developed by the "Father of Lacrosse." Beers and his Montreal Lacrosse Club "missionaries" would successfully transplant the game in Great Britain, Europe, Australia and other faraway lands, often sowing the seed through orchestrated tours featuring the best First Nations and Canadian players. The eastern United States fully embraced lacrosse in the 1870s and soon became the hotbed of university-level play.

The final section of the book, "The Stickmaker," pays homage to the artist who sees the possibility inherent in a piece of hickory, who creates the stick that is meant for the individual player, the stick that he will take with him when his time on Earth is through.

The Iroquois maintain that we are all related. The game in many ways ties together the various peoples who traded with each other, fought with and against one another, and worked together to form the new world. It has survived the turmoil of nation-building and reminds us of our shared past. It remains the Creator's game, and it is Lacrosse — The Ancient Game.

Jim Calder
PUBLISHER

PART I

The Oral Tradition

The Words of a Cayuga Faithkeeper

DAO JAO DRE

Greetings, I hope this message finds you in good health and fine spirits. My Ongwehonwe Haudenosaunee (Six Nations) name is Dao Jao Dre. It means "A Flat Prairie with a Raging Fire Coming Towards You Across the Horizon." My clan mother gave me this name in the midwinter ceremony in the longhouse fifty-four years ago. I am a member of the Cayuga Nation, within the Wolf clan. My English name is Delmor Jacobs.

Ongwehonwe Haudenosaunee means "original people building a longhouse." The Ongwehonwe Haudenosaunee Confederacy was originally comprised of five nations: the Onondaga, the Oneida, the Mohawk, the Seneca and the Cayuga. In 1721, the Tuscarora Nation was driven from the present-day Carolina area. They requested and found sanctuary with the Ongwehonwe Haudenosaunee Confederacy. Their adoption into the Confederacy resulted in the Six Nations Confederacy. Although the Confederacy has a wide area of influence, the original homelands are located in the Finger Lakes region of New York State and north of Lake Ontario into Canada.

I am also a Faithkeeper within the longhouse culture and have been since I was fourteen years old. The stories that I am going to tell you are my interpretation from my cultural background with the Ongwehonwe Haudenosaunee.

As a Faithkeeper, I am responsible for ensuring that our cultural ceremonies are performed correctly. I am part of a brotherhood of Faithkeepers with a single leader, a head Faithkeeper. There are also Faithkeepers on the female side of the longhouse with a similar structure. When ceremonies are nearing completion, the leader comes to all Faithkeepers to ensure the proper procedures were followed. If the ceremony was not properly performed or a procedure missed, my duty is to say "yea" or "nay" and to remind everyone of the missing part. If this occurs, the head Faithkeeper announces the point, the missing section is performed, and we are asked again. Once all the Faithkeepers have agreed, the ceremonies are closed. This is how we ensure that our ceremonies adhere to tradition.

The Creator's game is holistic. Besides being a game, it is considered to be medicine. In this manner we play the game to heal someone in our community, our families or for friendships.

OPPOSITE:
*Cayuga Faithkeeper
Dao Jao Dre
with Lacrosse Stick.*
Painting by David Craig

Clans of the Six Nations Confederacy

Within the Six Nations Confederacy, each nation is comprised of several clans. A clan is like an extended family and is based on a matrilineal system: a child belongs to the same clan as his or her mother. Traditionally, a person marries outside of their clan. Clans are divided into the three earth elements — land, air and water — then split into nine animal designations. The number of clans varies from nation to nation. For instance, the Mohawk have three, while the Onondaga have nine. And some clans, such as the Wolf and Turtle clans, are more popular than others, depending on the community.

LAND
Bear, Deer, Wolf

WATER
Beaver, Eel, Turtle

AIR
Hawk, Heron, Snipe

OPPOSITE: *Clan Circle*.
Painting by Arnold Jacobs

There is a game that is deeply engrained in our culture, and we call it "the Creator's game." Non-Native people call it lacrosse. I will explain why we call it the Creator's game and the reasons why it is so important to the Ongwehonwe Haudenosaunee.

The game stretches from cradle to grave for our people. Many young boys are given a small wooden lacrosse stick while they are still in the cradle. The stick is there at the other end, too. I have been to two funerals in the last little while, and both men were buried with their lacrosse sticks in their caskets. This is done so that they can play the game when they go to our Creator's world. I, too, have requested to take a stick with me when I pass from here.

The Creator's game is holistic. Besides being a game, it is considered to be medicine. In this manner, we play the game to heal someone in our community, our families or for friendships. After the game is completed, the ball is usually kept by the person who seeks the healing. In these situations, tobacco is burned. The burning of tobacco is how the spiritual world is contacted.

The Creator's game is played on reservations across the United States and Canada. Places such as Onondaga, Tonawanda, Cattaraugus, Kahnawake, St. Regis, Akwesasne, Tuscarora, and Oneida. Everyone plays it within their realm.

The Creator's game is traditionally played with wooden sticks. Traditional sticks are made out of hickory. There is a reason for the use of hickory, which I will get to later on. Some Native people made sticks from wood that was more readily available to them, such as ash, willow, etc.

I have said our traditional lands — our areas of influence — were around the Finger Lakes and beyond, but at one time our lands stretched halfway up the eastern seaboard, north to Ottawa, and west to the Ohio and Mississippi. We had a high level of control through the Six Nations and the Confederation. We became the role model for creating government in the New World. Each of our nations played a specific role.

A. JACOBS
©01

19

The Mohawk, Onondaga and Seneca are known as the "elder brothers," and the Cayuga, Oneida and Tuscarora are known as the "younger brothers." Together they form our government.

Before the Tuscarora returned north, the Mohawk were on the eastern side of New York State and were the "Keepers of the Eastern Door." The Onondagas remain the chairmen of the board of the Confederacy. The Oneida and the Cayugas' trait is a cognitive role within the Confederacy. The Seneca were the "Keepers of the Western Door," from Seneca Lake west to Buffalo.

Here is how things work. The Mohawk bring issues to the floor. The elder brothers talk about it and make a decision, then they pass it on to the younger brothers. The younger brothers talk about it and pass it on to the Onondagas. Once total consensus is achieved, the Onondagas report to the results.

Eel Clan

How North America Was Formed

In the beginning, before land and people were here on the Earth, there was a land above us, just above the clouds, we are told. There were lands, birds, animals and people up there — a land very similar to what we have on Earth. It was the Creator's land, and it is called the Skyworld.

In the Skyworld, there are many types of trees, and there existed a big central tree called the Tree of Light. There was a man who was given charge of taking care of the tree. We are told that eventually the man's wife became pregnant. During her pregnancy, she had cravings, so much so that she had dreams of creating a tea from the sacred tree's bark. These cravings led her to the central tree. The Skywoman wanted to make tea from the bark. When she went close to the tree, she could see there was something beneath the tree's roots. She was so curious, she wanted her husband to lift the tree up so that she could see what was under it. The man said he couldn't do this. Well, we all know the influence a wife has on a husband. He eventually gave in to her continuous requests.

He lifted the tree and underneath they could only see blackness. She bent over to look closer. Now, some say she was pushed and some say she fell. While attempting to stop her fall, she grabbed pieces of the Creator's land and brought them with her to the Earth. I will explain it further when we look at the good and the bad in the world.

OPPOSITE:

Deliverance of Sky Woman.
Painting by Arnold Jacobs

Beaver Clan

She was falling for some time. She heard whirling wind and saw water. There were waterfowl, and the waterfowl saw her falling. Some geese came to her rescue and lifted her up so she wouldn't hit the water, but they couldn't carry her forever. They saw a great sea turtle, who said, "Put her on my back." So they laid her gently on the back of the giant sea turtle. After resting, she asked if there was any earth in this world.

The aquatic animals said there was, but it was way under the water. The otter, the beaver and the muskrat tried to reach some and bring it to her. The beaver and the muskrat lost their lives in their attempts. When the otter came up, he too had died in the attempt, but he had a little earth in his paw. The Skywoman put the earth on the turtle's back and began to move around on it. As she moved upon it, it became bigger and bigger and bigger and soon covered the back of the sea turtle. That's why we refer to North America as Great Turtle Island. Many Native Americans you talk to still refer to North America as Turtle Island.

The dance that the Skywoman did is still performed in the longhouse today. It is called the Women's Shuffle dance. The women dance it as the men sing.

The Games of the Beginning
THE BATTLE BETWEEN GOOD AND EVIL

Skywoman gave birth to a female child. They both survived, and when the female child grew to childbearing age, she became pregnant. The Skywoman's daughter would eventually become our Mother Earth. This pregnancy was a big mystery, since there were no men around. When her mother, the Skywoman, asked how this had happened, the girl explained that within a dream she had dreamt of the West Wind. The West Wind had come to her and impregnated her by just touching her and placing two arrows across her stomach. One arrow was sharp and one arrow was dull. She became pregnant with twins. The significance between the dull arrow and the sharp arrow is that they would be direct opposites. One entity would emulate good, the other evil. We are told that the twins even fought within the womb.

As time went on, she gave birth. The first child was born in the correct way, and he was our Creator (known as Sapling, Teharonhiawakon, Holder of the Heavens). He created all things that are here on Earth. He was attractive to look at and held all attractive attributes.

And then Uncle (known as Flint, Sawiskera and Mischievous One), his twin brother, came out of his mother's side, from under her armpit, and killed his mother. By this action

Confrontation. Painting by Arnold Jacobs

First Nations' Names for the Game

Baaga'adowe   (Ojibwe)

Baggattaway   (Algonquin)

Da-na-wah'uwsdi   (Eastern Cherokee)

Dehuntshigwa'es   (Onondaga)

DeionTshihgwah:is   (Haudenosaunee)

Kabocha-toli   (Choctaw)

O-ta-da-jish-qua-age   (Iroquois)

Pa-ka-ha-to   (Manitoba)

Pa-ki-ta   (Mississippi)

Pe-ki-twe   (Upper Great Plains)

Teiontsesiksaheks   (Algonquin)

Tewaarathon   (Mohawk)

Turtle Clan

he became the evil twin. And so, when we look at things, we have our Creator, who is good, and his brother, our Uncle. Because he is our Uncle, he is connected, not separate, yet he killed his mother, so he is very evil.

The twins' mother was buried in the earth and became our Mother Earth. The Skywoman buried with her daughter the plants she brought from the Skyworld. From her daughter's head grew corn, beans and squash (the Three Sisters). Sacred tobacco grew from her heart, and from her feet, strawberry plants. Other plants and medicines grew from her as well.

The grandmother took responsibility for the twins, but she was old and mistakenly thought it was the good twin who had killed her daughter. Thinking this, she favored the bad twin in their upbringing. Upon her death, the twins argued about what to do with her body. During that argument, the bad twin grabbed the grandmother's head and flung it into the sky. Her head became the moon, and it helps to bring some light to her favored bad twin's dark world.

Eventually, the Creator made people on the Earth. Our Creator saw that Uncle wanted to control the people. This caused a disagreement. The Creator was of the good mind: he said, instead of killing each other outright, they should have a contest through games. Whoever won the game would win the world.

One of the games they agreed upon was called the Great Peach Bowl Game. And we still play it in our longhouse ceremonies today. It involves a bowl that is a foot wide and maybe four to six inches deep. It is very smooth. In this bowl are six peach pits. The peach pits are cleaned and carved so they wobble. The peach pits are colored white on one side for our Creator and dark on the other side for our Uncle.

An individual lifts up the bowl and moves it so that the peach pits bounce and settle. The object is to get it all light or all dark sides facing up. It is so unpredictable. I have seen games go for three days.

Today, the Great Peach Bowl Game is played in midwinter, midsummer and at maple syrup time. We mainly play against other clans. I'm a Wolf clan, but my wife is a Turtle clan, and all my children are Turtle clan because they follow their mother's clan — clans are matrilineal — so we play against each other, which is a lot of fun. All bets must be natural: turtle rattles, lacrosse sticks, wampum, different things you sing with, traditional clothing. So you bet these things through the Faithkeepers of your clan. They go to your house early in the morning and ask for the things you are going to bet. So from six to nine or ten in the morning, this is happening on the other side, as well. The Faithkeepers who gather the bets from both sides then meet and match the bets — lacrosse stick with lacrosse stick, or whatever.

When you win this game, you don't really win; and when you lose, you don't really lose. The winners are able to get back what they bet plus what was attached to it. If you lost, you will find that item waiting for you in the Creator's land when you get there. We say, "You send it ahead." All those things will be in our Creator's land when we get there.

Back when Uncle and Creator played, they did so for six days with no one winning. So the Creator came up with another game. It was a stickball game, and the only rule was that the players couldn't touch the ball with their hands. A stick was used between the hand and the ball. Originally, it was supposed to be a small stick, just long enough to keep the hand from the ball, but enabling control of the ball. A player would use his body to block the other

The Great Peach Bowl Game uses peach pits colored white on one side, for our Creator, and dark on the other side, for our Uncle.
Photograph by Jim Calder

players from the ball. So it was very important to have a healthy body in order to play the game. This was the beginning of lacrosse.

The rules were agreed upon. Even today, the rules are agreed upon within the various lacrosse organizations. The Creator and the Uncle played this game for six days and no one won. Our Uncle got tired of the games that ended in stalemates. Being the essence of evil, our Uncle wanted to just fight it out, so they agreed on it. Our Uncle grabbed the nearest thing, a spear. Our Creator picked up a deer's antler. It was the deer's antler that our Creator used to subdue our Uncle and put him under the earth. Our Uncle was designated to rule the night. Our Uncle now controls everything under the earth and his time is the nighttime. Our Creator's realm is the earthly plane and the daylight time. That's how good triumphed over evil and the deer antler became a symbol. These deer antlers are called the "horns of authority" because they symbolize overcoming evil. Iroquoian chiefs have these horns of authority within their bonnets, so you can tell immediately who is a chief. Chiefs are held in very high esteem among the people they serve.

This is the story of how the Creator invented the stickball game as a peaceful alternative to outright war. Upon European contact, the Great Lakes type of stick looked like a bishop's staff, and because of this, the game began being called "lacrosse."

Power Struggle. Painting by Arnold Jacobs

False Face and the Thunder Entities

Our Creator was looking over the world he had created when he ran across a particular being. He was kind of older-looking, with long hair. He had with him a hickory cane and a turtle rattle. Our Creator didn't know where he had come from. When our Creator asked who he was, the person said, "I am called Hadoui." He explained that he had been born out of the West Wind. Hadoui asked our Creator who had created this world. Our Creator told him that he had created this world. But Hadoui insisted that he, Hadoui, was the most powerful being in this world. Our Creator then asked Hadoui to show him his power.

Our Creator said, "Let's prove it through a contest. Off in the distance, there is a mountain. You must move the mountain." Hadoui began. He shook his rattle, began singing and hitting his cane on the earth. Pretty soon the mountain started to shake. It moved about halfway to them then stopped. Hadoui said, "There, I have shown you my power is great."

The Creator agreed that Hadoui's power was great. Then our Creator said, "OK, turn around." The Creator had moved the mountain to within inches of Hadoui. Hadoui was so anxious to see how far the mountain had moved that he turned around too quickly and ended up breaking his nose on the mountain. His broken nose was the result of him testing our Creator's power. One of the names by which we refer to Hadoui is "Old Broken Nose." He is also known as False Face.

Hadoui, False Face, agreed that our Creator had proven he was the most powerful being on the Earth. He said he would go back to where he came from, since he had lost the contest. The Creator asked him to stay and look after the people he was going to create here on Earth. He asked False Face to fight diseases through medicine and also to control the weather. Hadoui accepted the jobs and asked only that in exchange for his help, the people feed him and give him tobacco.

The traditional lacrosse stick is made from hickory, like False Face's cane. We are told that because False Face favors hickory trees, if you have hickory trees around your house,

Outside the longhouse, we place the sticks all in a circle, and in the middle of the circle we burn tobacco and we thank the Thunder Entities again for coming to clear the air.

Orenda

*An old-style lacrosse stick
is more than piece of wood.
Every time it is used, its power
increases. The Seneca call
this invisible power* **orenda**.
*It is generated by the good
thoughts and sportsmanlike
conduct of the player, and is
enhanced through the proper
use and care of the lacrosse stick.
The Haudenosaunee believe
the lacrosse stick is also a form
of medicine. Lacrosse is meant
to teach its players the lessons
of life. We will not always win,
but we should always seek to
please our people and our
Creator through excellent
and dignified performance
on the field.*

he won't send bad weather your way. If you were going to make a traditional stick, you would go to the edge of the woods and make an offering. These trees, like all medicines, are living entities. When you put down tobacco as an offering, they understand.

After offering tobacco, you will find the tree, the medicine, you are looking for. You could use other types of trees, but they are not as strong or flexible. Every tree has its particular job to do. That is why there are various types of trees. If they could all do every job, they would all be the same. Much like the Thunder Entities, who have their job to perform. The hickory tree's job is to make a lacrosse stick. We are told that a hickory tree hit by lightning is even more special for stickmaking.

The Seven Thunder Entities made their home at the thundering waters of Niagara Falls. More specifically, in the caves beneath the crashing waters. In their home, the Thunder Beings surrounded themselves with the holistics of water. All the aspects of water can be experienced at Niagara Falls. But we are told that this area became too polluted due to overpopulation, too many people took up residence too close to the Thunder Entities' home, and that is the reason they moved west.

During a thunderstorm, what is thrown by the Thunder Entities is like a flat stone, much like one you would skip across water. If you go where the earth or an object has been struck by lightning, and you are not afraid, and you move very quickly, you can find that stone. This stone will tell you when it is going to rain or when something is coming. The stone will become wet.

Hadoui also controls the weather and, as a part of that duty, works with the Seven Thunder Entities. The Thunder Entities bring the summer thunderstorms. When they come each spring, they are doing their job, clearing the air. The Thunder Entities also like to play the Creator's game in springtime.

Within the Cayuga Nation, we play a lacrosse game every springtime, in the middle of April. Our Creator and the Thunder Entities also play the game at that time. We designate a ceremonial game to honor them, give thanks and as a way of entertaining them. Outside the longhouse, we place all the sticks in a circle, and in the middle of the circle we burn tobacco and we thank the Thunder Entities again for coming to clear the air. Without this game, the whole universe would be in chaos.

The game is to seven goals. The goals are outlined, and the game is played with wooden sticks. When the seventh goal is scored, the game is over. The length of game depends on the enthusiasm of the players and the influence of the Thunder Entities, since it is for their entertainment.

When a thunderstorm goes through, you can feel the rough and tumble, like a lacrosse game. And also, after the rain goes by, it is so clean. Everything is refreshed with the rain and it is usually cooler. We are also told that the lightning and the thunder keep fierce creatures under the earth.

Places where the lightning has struck are sacred sites. When I was much younger, I went to Tonawanda to a sacred site during a drought. The whole longhouse was full of False Faces, and we all had to dance with them. We were told Our Grandfather, Hadoui, was there, too. When a special meeting is called by the False Faces, our Grandfather is always there. We went out of the longhouse and down the road to the site where a tree had been split by a bolt of lightning. We did a ceremony there, and within three days we got rain.

The False Face society helps heal through their ceremonies. They are highly respected for the jobs they perform on our behalf. False Face masks are carved from living trees. When the mask is cut out of the tree, the wound heals and the tree does not die. While performing their ceremonies, the False Faces handle ashes and red-hot coals with their bare hands. During all this, the coals never burn them. False Faces are connected to the weather and medicine. Because of this, they are also connected to the healing game of lacrosse.

FOUR WARRIORS PLAY A GAME

The oral tradition of the Haudenosaunee explains that when we walk the Skyroad path to the Skyworld, we will hear the people cheering at a lacrosse game.

Once there were four Haudenosaunee warriors who had made their way to the edge of the world. As they entered the Skyworld, they heard the cheering crowds and found that a lacrosse game was being played.

The referee was an older man. Every now and then, he would call out to the players and warn them to watch their conduct. There was one player who seemed to ignore the referee and kept up his dirty play. The referee warned him three times to stop such play, but his warnings were ignored. Finally, as the obstinate player raced by the referee, the old man reached out and grabbed him with surprising strength. The old man then flung the player so hard that he was driven through a tree and lodged there.

"Wait there for a while and think about what you have been doing," commanded the old man. "I told you not to play that way. That is not the way lacrosse is meant to be played!"

Slowly, the tree worked its wonder on the player. The power of the tree took away the player's anger and his need to hurt other players. It allowed his mind to realize that we are meant to respect one another.

When he finally realized why his actions were wrong, he was released from the tree and resumed his place on the lacrosse field. He never played dirty again. The other three players learned from this lesson as well.

The old man was the Creator. The tree represents the medicinal powers of wood. Old lacrosse sticks were made of hickory, which is also a form of medicine. In the spiritual teachings of the Haudenosaunee oral tradition, trees have life and power, and wood cut from the tree retains some of that life and power.

The Game Between the Birds and the Animals

Like many other nations, the Ongwehonwe Haudenosaunee share and teach cultural values through oral traditions. One of the most endearing lessons involves the Creator's game. This particular story teaches us that everyone is important, everyone has a particular talent, and these talents can make a difference in the final outcome of events.

The story goes like this. The four-legged animals and the winged animals wanted to play the Creator's game. The specific attributes or skills of a particular animal teammate would be used to win the game. For example, the bear's large size and great strength make him hard to stop; the deer possesses speed and grace; and the slow-but-sure turtle just keeps advancing. These traits could help the four-legged animals win. Similarly, the skills of the winged animals could help them win. The owl has excellent eyesight and can see in all directions; the eagle is known for his strength, including his ability to lift heavy things high into the air.

The bat wanted to play, too, and asked the four-legged animals to include him. But they didn't want him. They said he wasn't a four-legged and they refused him. He went to the birds, but they didn't want him either. They said, "You are an animal because you don't have any feathers." The bat just wanted to play. Eventually the birds said, "OK, we see that you can fly, awkwardly, so you can play on our team."

The game was really close, with each team member on both sides using their particular skill to advance the ball. The sides were so evenly matched, and the bat motioned time and time again for his teammates to pass the ball to him, but it never came. The match continued with both sides unable to score. Finally the feathered team agreed to let the bat try. The four-legged team couldn't match the unique flying ability of the bat, with its dipping and diving. They were unable to stop him, and the bat moved forward and scored. So it was that the bat's particular talent allowed him to score the winning goal. The story tells us that everyone should have the opportunity play and be involved and use their particular talents to influence the game's outcome.

The four-legged team couldn't match the unique flying ability of the bat, with its dipping and diving.

OPPOSITE:
Animal-Bird Game.
Painting by Arnold Jacobs

The Peacemaker, Ayenwatha and the Great Peace

Heron Clan

Deganawidah, the Peacemaker, was sent by our Creator to bring peace and harmony to the nations of Turtle Island. We are told he was born of the Huron Nation on the north shore of Lake Ontario as early as the early 1400s. In a dream, his mother was visited by a spirit who told her that her son was to deliver the Creator's message of peace to the people on Earth.

We are told that the young girl's mother tried to kill the baby in a number of ways, but each time the baby miraculously survived. Then, one night, a spirit visited the girl's mother's dreams and told her the baby had a special job to do in this world. He was to bring peace to the world. He was sent by the Creator, and she was not to interfere. The girl's mother ceased her actions and helped to raise the child.

The Peacemaker grew up as a normal boy but demonstrated many special abilities while becoming a young man. When he reached manhood, he announced that he would begin his mission. He built a canoe out of white stone and began his journey to the Haudenosaunee, located in today's New York State. He was sent to bring an end to the bloodshed of the warring nations.

Nearing the southern side of Lake Ontario, he met people whom were running away from their villages because of bloodshed there. The Peacemaker told them to return and tell the people of a message of peace from the Creator. These people saw the Peacemaker's stone canoe and realized he had special powers, so they left to deliver the message.

The Peacemaker continued on his journey and came to a crossroads. There was a woman's lodge there. The owner's name was Jikonsahsah. The woman would offer traveling hunters and warriors rest and good food. We are told she would then poison them and rob them of their goods.

The woman invited the Peacemaker in, thinking she had another victim. The Peacemaker told her she was to stop what she was doing and accept the Creator's message. Startled and afraid, she asked, "What is the message?"

The Peacemaker outlined the message: "All people shall love one another and live together in peace. Our Creator made all things for all his creation's benefit. The message

OPPOSITE:

Comes the Peacemaker.
Painting by Arnold Jacobs

33

The Meaning of the Six Nations' Names

MOHAWK
People of the Flint

ONONDAGA
People of the Hills

ONEIDA
People of the
Standing Stone

CAYUGA
People of the
Great Swamp

SENECA
People of the
Great Hill

TUSCARORA
The Hemp Gatherers

Wolf Clan

has three parts: Peace, Power and Righteousness. Peace begins in everyone who develops a sound mind and body. Righteousness comes from justice practiced between men and the nations they make. Power comes when we join together with the good mind. This is the will of our Creator."

Jikonsahsah accepted these words and said she would stop her evil ways and never bring harm to anyone again. The Peacemaker said that because she was the first to accept the message of Peace, Power and Righteousness, he would proclaim that women be given the title to chieftainships. Women would head the clans and choose who would become chiefs.

The Peacemaker then journeyed towards the sunrise to confront Ayenwatha (Hiawatha), an evil man who ate people. When the Peacemaker arrived at Ayenwatha's lodge, no one was there, but he soon heard someone approaching and climbed on the roof to observe the person.

The Peacemaker saw a man carrying a human body over his shoulder. The man entered the lodge and placed the body in a large boiling pot to prepare it for eating. The Peacemaker climbed to the smoke hole of the lodge and looked in. At the same time, Ayenwatha looked in the pot and saw the face of the Peacemaker reflected in the water of the pot. He immediately thought, "How could a man that looks like this do what I am doing?" Just looking at the Peacemaker's face began to change the mind of Ayenwatha.

The Peacemaker climbed down and they met. The Peacemaker instructed Ayenwatha to bury the dead people and eat deer meat instead. He taught him that the Creator had made animals for man to eat and that he was not to eat people. He also declared that the antlers of the deer were to be symbols of authority.

The Peacemaker taught Ayenwatha the Creator's message, and Ayenwatha accepted the Creator's message. The Peacemaker took away Ayenwatha's evil mind and replaced it with the good mind. He instructed Ayenwatha that he must go to the areas where he spread evil and fear and spread the message of peace.

Ayenwatha was the first man to accept the message of Peace, Power and Righteousness. Because of this, he became the first Sachem (Chief) of the Mohawk Nation. The Peacemaker then went to the rest of the Mohawk Nation.

When the Peacemaker met the Mohawks, they were doubtful and asked for proof. They instructed him to climb a tall tree near the edge of Cohoes Falls. They would cut the tree down into the gorge, and if he lived, they would accept his message. This was done, and the tree with the Peacemaker disappeared into the gorge. When the Mohawks did not see the Peacemaker arise, they thought that was the end of it. But the next morning, they saw smoke rise at the Peacemaker's camp. They found the Peacemaker unmarked and healthy, and they accepted his message.

While the Peacemaker went to the Mohawk Nation, Ayenwatha went to the Onondaga Nation, near today's city of Syracuse. The Onondaga Nation was ruled by an evil, dangerous man named Atotarho, who used sorcery, warfare and bad medicine to control his people. They were quite afraid of him. Atotarho ate people, had snakes in his hair and had seven crooks in his body. He was quite a sight to behold.

The Onondaga Nation wanted to accept the plan of peace, but Atotarho refused. He sent storms, treachery and bad omens to the people so they would stop trying to change his ways. Atotarho hired a sorcerer named Ohsinoh to get Ayenwatha to leave.

Ayenwatha had seven daughters. In Ongwehonwe Haudenosaunee culture, daughters are the future seed of every man. They bring life to the Earth and are highly respected for this quality. In order to make Ayenwatha leave, Ohsinoh caused the deaths of Ayenwatha's seven daughters. Ayenwatha fell into a deep depression and lost his mind. He became a wanderer. As he wandered, he

The Cultural and Spiritual Significance of Wampum

According to oral history of the Ongwehonwe Haudenosaunee, wampum was created by Ayenwatha (Hiawatha), who, with Deganawidah (The Peacemaker), delivered the Great Binding Law of Peace that began the Six Nations Confederacy. These purple and white quahog-shell beads were threaded together to form strings of beads. These strings were attached together to form "belts." The purple strands formed specific pictures in the belts that illustrated the words of treaties. Earlier forms of wampum were made of knotted reeds or from the dried, cored sumac plant. Wampum beads/strings possessed the power to relieve spiritual pain and cure severe emotional losses by clearing the sufferer's mind and being and connecting it to the Creator.

Wampum also served as a promissory notes, much in the same way Europeans used paper contracts, agreements, treaties, even marriage certificates. Nations, clans, organizations and individuals used wampum strings and belts to solidify spoken agreements and to establish the honor of those involved.

Realizing the value that First Nations people placed on wampum, seventeenth-century European traders began using the sacred items as money. This questionable practice was halted in the New England colonies in 1660s but remained active in various other settlements until the early eighteenth century.

approached a small lake. And because his mind was so cloudy, he didn't care if he entered the water and drowned. Our Creator caused a large flock of ducks to land on the water and quickly fly away. There were so many ducks that when they landed and flew away, they took the water with them. Instead of walking into a lake, Ayenwatha walked onto a dry lakebed. He crossed the lakebed and gathered white and purple shells. Once across the lake, he made his camp. He began to string these shells and said that if he found anyone in deep grief, he would use these strings of beads to console them, to lift their minds and take away the darkness.

Ayenwatha had invented wampum. When the Peacemaker met Ayenwatha again, he used wampum to console him and re-establish his mind. The Peacemaker and Ayenwatha used wampum to establish the Great Law of Peace.

The Peacemaker and Ayenwatha eventually succeeded in changing Atotarho. They are said to have combed the snakes from is hair and straightened the seven crooks in his body. This symbolized Atotarho's transition from evil to good.

The Peacemaker and Ayenwatha also brought together the Mohawk, Onondaga, Oneida, Cayuga and Seneca to accept the Great Law of Peace. The Peacemaker established all the rules and protocols and formatted these through the wampum strings and belts. Even today, clan mothers hold officially sanctioned strings of wampum as official symbols of their titles.

Bear Clan

Handsome Lake and Lacrosse in Heaven

The late eighteenth century saw devastating effects of European contact. The Ongwehonwe Haudenosaunee league was diminishing. Lands and hunting grounds were being lost. Disease and alcohol were talking a toll. This was the world in which Handsome Lake lived.

Handsome Lake was born in 1735 at Conawagas, on the Genesee River, in Livingston County, near Avon, New York, and given the name Shaking Snow. He was of the Turtle clan. His chief's name, given to him in middle age, was Ganio'dai'io or Ska'nidario', which translates as "Handsome Lake."

As a chief, his name appears on treaties made at the time. Later in his life, when the Genesee lands were lost, Handsome Lake and the Seneca Nation moved to the Allegany River area. At this time, he is said to have been past his prime and of average attributes. We are

OPPOSITE:

Vision of Handsome Lake.
Painting by Arnold Jacobs

Cornplanter,
brother of Handsome Lake.
Portrait by Frederick Bartoli, 1796

told that "he was a victim of the drink," and he became bedridden and helpless. He was poor, destitute. His daughter took care of him, and for four years he laid in bed as an invalid. But his condition provided him time to reflect on his life and the conditions around him.

He began to think of the natural world. He experienced the night with its stars and its noises, and the morning sun, with the birds singing and the fresh smell of morning dew. He pondered why this world existed and who had created all things. He thought of his position as the people's leader. He thought, "There must be a reason why all this was created and why am I a part of it. What does this mean?"

He began to remember what he was told as a young man. He had been told how firewater would destroy the people. He remembered who he was, his relationship to our Creator, Shongway a' dihs: on ("He Who Created You"), and how everything in creation was related to each other and to our Creator. He began to give thanks for seeing each morning and for enduring each night. He gave thanks for the sunlight, air, trees and the beautiful songs of the various birds. He began to invoke the good mind in himself and found himself getting stronger.

But he had a relapse when he let bad thoughts enter his mind. The bad thoughts flung him back to illness. He found he needed to rekindle his relationship with our Creator and his people. This was the only way he could help his people survive. So he did.

On a June morning, Handsome Lake's daughter and husband were readying beans for planting when she heard her father exclaim, "Niio'!" ("So be it!"). They heard him rise from his bed and walk to the door and saw him then collapse. They took him back to his bed and prepared him for burial. The daughter sent her husband to tell his brother, Giaint'waka ("Cornplanter"), and other relatives.

The husband went first to Handsome Lake's nephew, Taa'wonyas, ("Needle" or "Awl Breaker," one of the fifty sachems) and told him. Taa'wonyas arrived first. He touched the old man's body and discovered a warm spot over his chest. He told everyone to hold their grieving as Handsome Lake may yet rise. When Giaint'waka arrived, he too found the warm spot, but said nothing and sat down with everyone else.

Eventually, Taa'wonyas checked the body again and found the warm spot spreading. At noontime, a pulse was discovered and finally a breath, as well. Handsome Lake opened his eyes. Taa'wonyas asked him if he was well, and Handsome Lake tried to talk but only mouthed words, nothing came out. A short while later, Taa'wonyas again asked, "Are you well?" This time, Handsome Lake responded, "Yes, I think myself well."

First, Handsome Lake took a medicinal drink made by specified medicine people and held the strawberry ceremony. Once these instructions were performed, he then said, "Never have I witnessed such wondrous visions." He began to relate his experience. He said he was called out of his lodge. He heard this three times, so he rose and went outside. He said he saw three beings in a clearing a short distance away. He said the men were dressed in very fine clean clothing and had only a few feathers in their bonnets and had painted cheeks. They all seemed middle-aged and very handsome, the essence of commanding men. They held bows and arrows like canes in one hand and huckleberry branches with berries of all colors. Their feet never touched the ground.

The messengers showed Handsome Lake the past, present and the future of Native peoples of the world. They showed him how men spoiled the ways the Creator made for all life to live in harmony with each other. They showed him good and evil, the rewards and punishments of both.

The messengers then took Handsome Lake on the Skyroad. Handsome Lake was asked to look in a certain direction. Upon his observation the messengers asked him what he saw. He told them what he saw and they interpreted the vision's meanings.

On the Skyroad, he had a great many visions. Each revealed messages he was to take back to his relatives. When he neared the Creator's land, he came upon a grassy clearing with small trees and bushes. Here, he heard a voice. The voice said there would be a lacrosse game the next morning and that Awenhen: seh ("New Flower") would take the face-off. Handsome Lake knew the voice was that of his friend Johahi: seh. Johahi: seh had been dutiful in his earthly life and had carried on his leadership ways in the Creator's land. Handsome Lake also knew Awenhen: seh, but at the time of his collapse, Awenhen: seh was still among the living.

Gravesite of Handsome Lake.
Photograph by Jim Calder

Hawk Clan

Only upon his earthly revival did Handsome Lake learn that Awenhen: seh had passed away the previous day. Awenhen: seh was now in the Creator's land, where he took the face-off as predicted.

Before his return to Earth, Handsome Lake asked to see our Creator. He was told that, should he see the Creator, he would not be allowed to return home to his family. He was also told that his lodge awaited him in the Creator's land, but should he enter it now, he would be unable to return to Earth. Handsome Lake asked how long he had to deliver the good messages before traveling the Skyroad again. He was told he would be given three songs that he would receive at different times while delivering the messages. He was also told that after he received and sang the third song, and when the people gathered to play a lacrosse game to entertain him, then very shortly he would depart on his journey to the Creator's land.

Handsome Lake presented the Gai'wiio ("good word") with Cornplanter for ten years, then continued at Coldsprings for two years, and then at Tonawanda for four more. He was invited to go to the Onondaga Nation to speak the Gai'wiio. The messengers visited him again and gave instructions on how to prepare himself for the journey. Handsome Lake received the third song as he traveled to the Onondaga Nation. His followers were of greater number than usual because he told them he would soon journey to the Creator's land. But at Onondaga, he was ill and unable to present the Gai'wiio. The people gathered and carried him outside, where they would play a lacrosse game for him to lighten his spirits.

So, for sixteen years, until his death on August 15, 1815, Handsome Lake spoke the Gai' wiio. After he died, his message began to die too, and many began to return to alcohol and its violent ways. It was the Seneca women who inspired the men to revive his message. Now, every year, in the fall, it is presented at the reservations/reserves of the Ongwehonwe Haudenosaunee.

This has been an overview of the Ongwehonwe Haudenosaunee culture. I have presented a snapshot of some of the cultural uniqueness in relation to the Creator's game and its meaning to our people. Other Native nations have their unique origins of the sport of lacrosse. The Creator's game has been ingrained within our culture and communities forever. I hope you have enjoyed the readings.

Respectfully,
Dao Jao Dre
Delmor Jacobs

Deer Clan

PART II

Beyond the Native American Experience

A Recorded History

BRÉBEUF

The excitement had been growing all week in Ossossane. Everyone, from the wisest elder right down to the youngest child, anticipated the lacrosse game with the neighboring Ihonataria village that would end the four-day Feast of the Dead. The time of mourning was over. The responsibilities of the living to the souls of the ancestors had at last been discharged. The time approached for joyous celebration in the great game. Only a few grey clouds spoiled an otherwise sunny day.

The location of the field where the game would be played had just been announced, and people were bringing their wagers. Beaver pelts, robes and sacks of corn were piled on a frame at midfield. Soon tomahawks were added to the pile, along with beadwork, clothes and pipes. The crowd of spectators would be the largest many had ever seen. Other Wendat villages had sent players. It was considered a great honor to be selected to take the field, and for some this would be their first game.

But the game would be special for other reasons. There were many more bones than usual in the burial pit, and many more relatives had wailed with grief as loved ones were laid to rest. This game would go a long way toward restoring the community's spirits. The shaman had called the game for precisely this reason. He had said that a great cure was needed for the pestilence that raged through the land. Indeed, among the gathering crowd one could see the pockmarked faces of the sick as they were carried forward on litters.

There was also a new face, that of the giant "Black Robe," the Jesuit priest called Echon, known to the French as Jean de Brébeuf. Some claimed that the plague had begun when the Black Robes arrived, and that they were its cause. Certainly the medicine man believed Brébeuf held evil sorcerer's powers. Many of the children were afraid of the giant priest. Others, as they lay dying, asked that Brébeuf pray for them, as his god promised eternal life in heaven.

The Black Robe called the game "La Crosse," as its stick reminded him of a bishop's staff, la crosse d'évêque.

OPPOSITE:
Brébeuf Sees His First Huron Lacrosse Game, 1637.
Painting by David Craig

Jean de Brébeuf, aka "Echon".

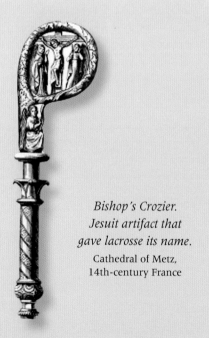

Bishop's Crozier.
Jesuit artifact that
gave lacrosse its name.
Cathedral of Metz,
14th-century France

The Black Robe called the game "La Crosse," as its stick reminded him of a bishop's staff, *la crosse d'évêque*.

It was in an effort to understand his ministry that Brébeuf had come to see this Feast of the Dead and its "lacrosse" game. In France, he had seen civilized tennis matches in which rackets were used, but this promised to be a far more violent game. The participants' immodest dress and aggressive behavior strained his tolerance as a man of God.

To ensure the spirits would take a close interest in the game, the medicine man insisted that correct procedures be followed. He made sure that the men were among the Bear Clan's most fit. He instructed the players to sleep separate from their wives before the match. He took them to the place by the creek where they splashed themselves with water in purification rituals. The bark of the red willow had been gathered carefully and made into a cleansing drink still used today.

The crowd cheered their favorites as the players took to the field. These men were the pride of Ossossane. Some, seeking greater speed and agility, had tied bird feathers to their sticks. Others, hoping for additional strength, had affixed bear claws. One player had an owl's beak for clearer eyesight, another a bat's wings for the power to dart to and fro. All had smeared their arms and loins with the shaman's ointments. Children in the crowd carried miniature lacrosse sticks, hoping some day to follow in the steps of their heroes.

Draped in his beaver-skin robes, the medicine man had left his lodge earlier that morning and walked the length and breadth of the field in the grey mist, *okis* in hand to cast spells on the opposition and to bring good luck to his village. Among other things, he used a turtle shell rattle and an odd, twisted shape of wood. He chanted special songs. What more could he do?

He knew the Black Robe medicine was powerful — a vision dream had warned him. And just that spring, the French ships had brought with them two strange new creatures. One could catch the mice that destroyed the corn. It came to you when you called its name. The second crowed as the sun rose, praying to the spirit of the dawn.

Yet his people wanted the trade goods offered by the French — the pre-shaped iron hatchets and knives that never broke or wore out, the guns that killed game at a distance. Some of his people were living closer to the white man's mission in order to have access to such items. But these people were foolish.

The rising noise of the crowd, brought his attention back to the great game about to begin.

With great whoops the players made their way to midfield for the toss-up. The tallest of the Ossossane villagers was there, the pride of the people. When the ball was tossed, he leapt high to capture it in the webbing of his stick. The game was on!

After a few steps, he was surrounded by several opposing braves, but with a dramatic over-the-head action, he whipped the ball a great distance to a waiting team member. Sticks whacked against the new carrier, but he broke free. With a mighty toss, the hero parted the uprights. The Ossossane team had scored the first goal. Great cheering erupted from all sides. This was a great start. Surely, the Creator must favor them today. Even the sick wore satisfied smiles.

Brébeuf, however, was not smiling. He noted that the scorer had received a nasty gash to his leg and had to be helped to his feet. Such brutal activity might be entertaining, but certainly God would not be disposed to intervene in the lives of these simple folk by such bloodthirsty behavior.

The match continued. The players showed amazing speed as they chased the ball and tremendous skill in scooping it up with exact twists of the stick. Runners dodged and weaved, faking one way then suddenly going the other to avoid their pursuers. The players were clever. They were strong. They possessed great skills. The medicine man was proud. He noted that the spectators were intent on the game, cheering as a favorite broke free to head downfield.

At this point, the play moved to the distant side of the field, and the ball went missing in a patch of tall grass. Brébeuf's mind wandered. Were not the Jesuits doing their best to understand these people? It had been a full twenty-one years since Father Le Caron said the first mass near here in 1615, but the Huron had kept to their traditional ways.

Typical
Lacrosse Balls

Early 1800s

Wood

Deerskin

© Canadian Museum of Civilization

Mohawk
vs
Seneca
1797

In 1797, Col. William Stone wrote of a lacrosse game between the Mohawk and Seneca nations played at the Grand River reserve in Ontario:

"The combatants numbered about six hundred upon a side. The goals, designated by a pair of byes, were 30 rods [175 feet] apart and the goals of each pair about 30 feet apart. Each passage of the ball between them counted a point, but tally chiefs were allowed to check or curtail the count in order to protract the game. The ball was put into play by a beautiful girl."

Now the ball was found and a tall youth from Ihonatiria broke free from the pack. His speed gave him a clear run, and with a deft flick of his wrists, he brought the score even. The spectators appreciated such skill even though shown by a rival.

The game continued, scores were traded and the match went to three goals each. It had been agreed that the game would end when one side scored four goals, so the excitement was high. Although the wagerers would retrieve lost goods in the afterlife, they still wanted to win and continue to enjoy them here.

Suddenly the ball bounced across the field and dribbled to a stop at Brébeuf's feet. Because his fellow spectators had given him such a wide berth, Brébeuf found himself alone with the ball momentarily. Before anyone could recover it, the Black Robe bent down and picked it up. Brébeuf was an exceptionally large man, but he lobbed the ball back into play with a surprisingly awkward motion.

No one in the assembly failed to notice this shocking action. Except for two loud men who were intoxicated on some French alcohol, the crowd grew silent. It is said that when Brébeuf closed his hand on the ball, a thick cloud covered the sun. Some say the west wind picked up, as well. The medicine man shuddered.

But the players, intent on the action, quickly resumed their sport. The first to arrive tried to scoop up the ball, but it squirted from his stick. A scramble ensued. No one was able to capture the elusive ball. Players piled on. One player emerged with it but did not get far before he was slashed and tripped up. A wrestling match began. Fights broke out. Players struck sticks against sticks, and broken pieces of hickory wood soon littered the field. An unexpected and unseasonal rain began. The field muddied. Bits of dislodged feathers could be seen in the grass.

There would be no winner here today. The sick were taken to shelter as the rain became a downpour. The rest of the spectators followed. Finally, even the players ran from the field.

The medicine man stood alone in the rain.

In the distance he caught a last glimpse of a Black Robe. He could not help but feel that the turn of events was the work of that evil sorcerer.

Fort Michilimackinac

It was June, but a cold, fresh wind blew in from the Straits of Mackinac and whistled through the open gate of palisaded Fort Michilimackinac. The women gathered by the wooden gate wrapped their blankets more tightly around themselves. But warmth was not the only reason for this action. Hidden beneath the blankets were weapons of war: tomahawks, war clubs and knives. A game of lacrosse — the "little brother of war" — was about to begin, and this game would have dire consequences for some of its spectators.

It was time to celebrate King George III's birthday, and high atop the fort the British flag flew triumphantly in the breeze. The French soldiers had surrendered Quebec, and the flag of France had been lowered. The winds of change were not blowing favorably for French traders still plying the northwest.

And for the Natives, this change of rule was nothing short of disaster. The new British rulers treated them like subjects, not partners in trade. The age-old practice of gift-giving in return for trade rights was cancelled. The price of goods was raised. No gunpowder would be traded. Livelihoods were endangered. What could be done? How could these rude occupiers be driven from the land they so disrespected?

There was unrest throughout the northwest in 1763. The French had no right to turn over Native lands to the British. Neolin, the Delaware prophet, preached that this evil had resulted from leaving the path. The people must return to tradition and follow the time-honored rituals.

Various tribes formed their own ideas as to how to respond to the British. When Pontiac laid siege to Detroit, others drew courage. At Michilimackinac, Ojibwe war chief Minweweh, "The One with the Silver Tongue," created the plan for a deadly lacrosse game: "Our brothers, the Sauk, are willing to help with this. We will tell the soldiers that an important rematch is to be played, and that it will honor their king. They will be relaxed in their duties. Drink will flow. There will be heavy wagering on the outcome."

Gambling was very popular at lacrosse games. It showed the strength of your support for your team and your confidence in their success. Those who had lost in previous matches sought to recoup their loses. Previous winners sought to increase their spoils.

In the days leading up to the contest, the fort had experienced a run on certain types of trade goods. Tomahawks were in special demand, noted Alexander Henry, a young trader new to the fort. He was told they were popular items when wagering on lacrosse games, but a wise observer may have wondered why more expensive goods were being ignored.

By the time the match started, all his customers had gone and his trading room was empty, so, like the other traders and several of the soldiers, Henry turned his attention to the action outside the fort. Through his window, he could see the game in its early stages.

He watched as some of the women standing in the shade along the fort wall made wagers with beads or trade cloth. Some had babies on their backs, but several were huddled by the fort's gate with only a partial view of the field, which stretched all the way to the cold waters of the strait.

Though new to Fort Michilimackinac, Henry was not unfamiliar with lacrosse. He had seen the youth prepare their sticks, bending the white ash ends into circles after soaking them in large kettles of steaming water. The pocket on the end was about four inches or so in diameter and secured by rawhide binding. Since the wooden balls were also about four inches in diameter, there wasn't much extra room in the pocket. The ball fit snugly, so that it would remain securely cradled during a player's run. But you could get a good, powerful throw with it. A two-handed overhead shot was best, both accurate and strong.

Henry had observed that many of these sticks were decorated with designs similar to those found on ceremonial drumsticks and war rattles, including deep serrated grooves on their handles. But these ornate sticks appeared to be mostly for show, not for game use, where they might end up broken and discarded.

Earlier that day, he had watched the players use bear grease, charcoal and white clay to decorate their bodies. It was a form of personal and team identification. They used a partially burnt twig to carefully apply the mixture. You could also tell your teammate by the way his hair was prepared or what feathers were used.

An Ojibwe youth scored, and there was much enthusiastic shouting and pumping of arms, except by the blanket-wrapped women gathered near the gate. They yelled and cheered but otherwise showed little physical enthusiasm, their arms held steady at their sides. Henry thought it somewhat unusual when a second Ojibwe goal, giving them a commanding lead, failed to bring much reaction from the women.

Then the Sauk made a thrilling comeback, scoring twice to even the score. More and more soldiers left the fort to witness the spirited activity outside.

At this point, Henry felt a tug on his arm. It was Panis, the young slave girl of trader Charles de Langlade. She led Henry to the larger house next door. She was insistent. What was this all about, at such a critical point in the game?

OPPOSITE:
Fort Michilimackinac and the Lacrosse Ruse.
Painting by David Craig

No sooner had Henry reached the threshold of the adjacent house than he saw the lacrosse ball roll inside the fort. Several players rushed through the gates in hot pursuit, led by Madjeckewiss, an Ojibwe chief who could run like the wind despite his large size.

In a move that caught everyone by surprise, the players suddenly dropped their sticks and grabbed the war clubs and tomahawks that had been hidden beneath the women's blankets.

As Henry scrambled up the stairs to the attic, he could hear all mayhem break lose in the yard outside. Cries and screams were everywhere. Through a crack in the walls, he saw a British soldier stumble and fall, a dark crimson patch of blood soaking through his jacket. Another soldier was dragged down as he desperately tried to flee.

Henry was fortunate to survive that day and tell his tale. Although civilians and traders were spared, many soldiers lay dead.

Though neither Ojibwe nor Sauk scored a winning goal, they would never forget this day. Indeed, this match would go down as one of the most noteworthy in history. Some say that team sports are a substitute for real war, but never again would the sport be so directly a part of war.

The National Game

George Beers loved lacrosse. His father had taken him to Caughnawaga (Kahnawake), the reserve at the south end of the Montreal bridge, to see the Mohawk play the game. He had been only six years old at the time, but the sport had fascinated him and became a lifelong passion. Lots of people followed cricket, baseball or hockey, but young Beers knew lacrosse was the sport for him. It had not been imported from some distant land; it had originated right near where he lived.

Beers played the game from an early age, and in 1860 the seventeen-year-old was selected as one of two goalkeepers to play for the Montreal Lacrosse Club in an exhibition match with the Caughnawaga First Nations for the visiting Prince of Wales, Queen Victoria's eldest son, Prince Edward. Though less than two years older than the teenage Beers, the Prince was the first member of the British royal family to tour North America. The historic alliance between Great Britain and the Ongwehonwe Haudenosaunee resulted in many royal visits over the years.

OPPOSITE:
*Mohawk Lacrosse Rules
Taught to Dr. Beers.*
Painting by David Craig

1834
Exhibition Match

In 1834, a group of Montreal businessmen brought lacrosse players from the Mohawk villages of Caughnawaga (Kahnawake) and Akwasasne to play exhibition matches for crowds of curious spectators. These players were probably the best in the world, and these matches would lead to momentous changes in the world of lacrosse.

The initial exhibition match was played on the infield of the racetrack at Ville St. Pierre. For the first time, players had to remain within defined boundaries instead of being able to elude their pursuers by running off in all directions. Further, each team was allowed only seven players, so even though the field was much smaller than in the traditional Native game, a runner had to dodge fewer opponents in effort to move downfield. And since it was easier to get in the clear, there were more open players to receive passes.

Those who lamented these changes noted that this game involved far fewer members of the community. Also, where was the suspense of a runner disappearing into the woods only to emerge in an entirely different spot? And where were the scrums and the wrestling matches for the ball — the feats of strength, toughness and dogged determination?

In many ways, this revised game was a different sport than the traditional Native game. It was far removed from the Iroquois *tewaarathon* that involved the whole community in games played to heal the sick, honor the dead or substitute for war.

For better or worse, the evolution and growth of the game had begun.

Beers' enthusiasm for lacrosse was further amplified by the wave of nationalist fervor that would soon lead to the creation of a new country. It seemed as if the world had come to Montreal's door. Together, they put him at the center of an exciting world. He was a part of it all.

He was still seventeen when he wrote and published standardized rules for the game of lacrosse. According to Beers' Rules, the stick could be any length, but the ball was to be made of India rubber sponge with a circumference of between eight and nine inches. The length of the field could be agreed upon by the teams' captains, but he recommended it be two hundred yards long. Goals were to have two posts, six feet high and six feet apart, with flags on top. The crease was to extend six feet in front of each goal and could not be entered by an opponent unless the ball passed into it first. Teams were to be limited to twelve players, with no substitutions, even in the event of injuries. The positions were goalkeeper, point, cover point, center, and home fielders. Matches were best-of-five, the team with three goals being the winner. Ends were to be changed after each score. Spiked shoes were prohibited, as were throwing the stick and holding, striking, hitting or threatening of the opposition. The goalie was the only player allowed to use his hands to touch the ball.

On the Native reserves, whole villages would sometimes participate in sprawling games. Beers' Rules enabled him to play the game on a smaller scale with his friends. Beyond the reserves, it made sense to limit the number of players per side.

Montreal Lacrosse Club, Quebec, 1858.
McCord Museum

Montreal Lacrosse Club, Quebec, 1867.
McCord Museum

CANADA'S GAME

There's a new anthem on *Hockey Night in Canada*. Its composer won a nationwide contest with a song entitled "It's Canada's Game," which includes swirl of bagpipes and the voice of Foster Hewitt. But is hockey Canada's game?

For the longest time, most people thought lacrosse was Canada's national game — even before Montrealer George Beers codified the rules. It remained that way until 1964, when MP Jack Roxburgh discovered there was no record of Parliament ever having passed legislation to make lacrosse the national game.

As a former president of the Canadian Amateur Hockey Association, Roxburgh took special interest in this fact. He saw an opportunity to make hockey the nation's "official" sport.

In 1965 he introduced a private member's bill for Commons debate. British Columbia MP Robert Prittie, a former lacrosse champion, countered with his own bill. The battle was on.

You would have thought Parliament was debating a declaration of war. So many speakers wanted to wade in with their opinions that the time for debate ended without a decision.

It would be almost thirty years before the controversy was settled — in a typically Canadian way. In April of 1994, Bill C-212, claiming hockey as the country's national sport, was again put forward. And again lacrosse was counter-nominated.

The result? Compromise. Hockey became Canada's official winter sport, and lacrosse its summer game.

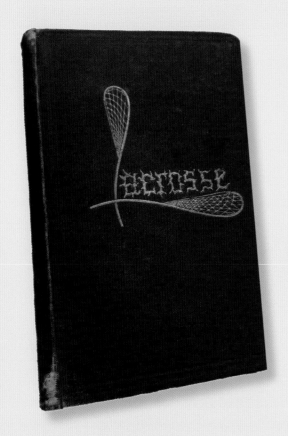

Original William George Beers book,
Lacrosse: The National Game of Canada.
© Canadian Museum of Civilization

With fewer players, you couldn't expect to cover the same distances as in the traditional Native contest. This new standardized game would require less running and encourage more passing — an approach that served his purposes rather well, as he felt his friends lacked the wind and stamina of the Natives. Players were assigned to cover specific areas of the field, and positions and roles were given names. This refined version of the game appealed to Beers' friends, who now hoped to compete with First Nations teams.

The newly defined sport of lacrosse took off. In 1867, Canada's year of confederation, it seemed like a new lacrosse club started up almost every week.

"Lacrosse is always fresh and lively, and sustains its attractiveness from beginning to end, no player has either time or inclination to sit on his heels and yawn," wrote Beers. "There is none of that serious work and gloomy pleasure which is the bane of some field games and which some players try to counteract by light gymnastics, or feats which have nothing to do with the game. It unbends the mind better than any other sport, because of the ubiquity of the ball; it is more genuine recreation, and is a holiday to the blood to play, and a half-holiday to look on."

Beers wanted everyone to get behind his game: "Gouty old gentlemen forget their big toes in the excitement of watching a struggle for the ball; the faces of crusty bachelors soften into the old smiles of their youth, while low grumbling laughter, as if afraid to come up, begins to shake them in epigastric regions, and gradually expanding into hearty haw-haws, gives them a permanent and happy cure.

"It seems very pardonable to enjoy the laughable shipwreck of some overweening dodger and his excited checker who make battering rams of their bodies, and send dodger, checker, crosses and ball all in a heap.

"Prudes forget their primness; snobs their propriety; old women fearlessly expose themselves to dismantling; young ladies to the demolishment of crinoline and waterfall; small boys to the imminent fracture of limb, dogs will rush frantically over the field and after the ball."

BEERS' RULES

THE GAME

RULE I — The Crosse.
Sec. 1 — The Crosse may be of any length to suit the player; woven with cat-gut...In its widest part the crosse shall not exceed one foot....

RULE II — The Ball.
The Ball must be India rubber sponge, not less than eight and not more than nine inches in circumference....

RULE III — The Goals.
The Goals may be placed at any distance from each other, and in any position agreeable to the captains of both sides. The top of the flag-poles must be six feet above the ground, including any top ornament, and six feet apart....

RULE IV — The Goal-Crease.
There shall be a line or crease, to be called the Goal-Crease, drawn in front of each goal, six feet from the flag-poles....

RULE V — Umpires.
Sec. 1 —There must be two umpires at each goal, one for each side, who must stand behind the flags when the ball is near or nearing the goal....
Sec. 2 — No umpire shall, either directly or indirectly, be interested in any bet upon the result of the match....
Sec. 3 — When "foul" has been called, the umpires must leave their posts and cry "time," and from that time the ball must not be touched by either party....

RULE VI — Referee.
The umpires shall select a referee, to whom all disputed games and points, whereon they are a tie, may be left for decision, and who must be thoroughly acquainted with the game, and in every way competent to act....

RULE VII — Captains.
Captains, to superintend the play, may be appointed by each side, previous to the commencement of a match....

RULE VIII — Names of Players.
The players of each side shall be designated as follows: "Goal-keeper," who defends the goal; "Point," first man out from goal; "Cover-point," in front of Point; "Centre," who faces; "Home," nearest opponent's goal. Others shall be termed "Fielders."

RULE IX — Miscellaneous.
Sec. 1 — Twelve players shall constitute a full field....
Sec. 2 — A match shall be decided by the winning of three games out of five, unless otherwise agreed upon.

(· · ·)

Sec. 6 — No Indian must play in a match for a white club, unless previously agreed upon.
Sec. 7 — After each game, the players must change sides.
Sec. 8 — No change of players must be made after a match has commenced....

RULE X — Spiked Soles.
No player must wear spiked soles.

RULE XI — Touching the Ball with the Hand.
The ball must not be touched with the hand....

RULE XII — Goal-Keeper.
Goal-keeper, while defending goal within the goal-crease, may pat away with his hand or block the ball in any manner.

RULE XIII — Ball in an Inaccessible Place.
Should the ball lodge in any place inaccessible to the crosse, it may be taken out by the hand....

RULE XIV — Ball Out of Bounds.
Balls thrown out of bounds must be picked up with the hand, and "faced" for at the nearest spot within the bounds.

RULE XV — Throwing the Crosse.
No player shall throw his crosse at a player or at the ball under any circumstances.

RULE XVI — Accidental Game.
Should the ball be accidentally put through a goal by one of the players defending it, it is game for the side attacking that goal. Should it be put through a goal by any one not actually a player, it shall not count.

RULE XVII — Balls Catching in the Netting.
Should the ball catch in the netting, the crosse must immediately be struck on the ground so as to dislodge it.

RULE XVIII — Rough Play, &c.
No player shall hold another with his crosse, nor shall he grasp an opponent's stick with his hands, under his arms, or between his legs; nor shall any player hold his opponent's crosse with his crosse in any way to keep him from the ball until another player reaches it. No player shall deliberately strike or trip another, nor push with the hand; nor must any player jump at to shoulder an opponent, nor wrestle with the legs entwined so as to throw his opponent.

RULE XIX — Threatening to Strike.
Any player raising his fist to strike another, shall be immediately ruled out of the match.

RULE XX — Foul Play.
Sec. 1 — Any player considering himself purposely injured during play, must report to his captain, who must report to the umpires, who shall warn the player complained of.
Sec. 2 — In the event of persistent fouling, after cautioning by the umpires, the latter may declare the match lost by the side thus offending, or may remove the offending player or players, and compel the side to finish the match short-handed.

RULE XXI — Interrupted Matches.
In the event of a match being interrupted by darkness or to any other cause considered right by the umpires, and one side having won two games — the other none — the side having won the two games shall be declared winners of the match....

RULE XXII — Amendments.
Any amendment or alteration proposed to be made in any part of these laws, shall be made only at the Annual Conventions of the National Association, and by a three-fourths vote of the members present.

Selected excerpts from "Laws of Lacrosse," *Lacrosse: The National Game of Canada*, by William George Beers, 1869.

Beers was proud to be a man of his age — an age in which everything could be improved by the application of a reasoned, scientific approach. Look at how the workplace had changed. Factories produced more and better goods for more people. We had steam engines, railways, cities! Civilization was changing the world. Sports must change, too. A reasoned approach was essential. A team with a well-thought-out plan could and would triumph over an undisciplined, if enthusiastic, attack. And the emphasis on passing was a big part of this improved strategy. The Native scrum demonstrated individual strength and courage, but how much more effective it was to just pass the ball to an open teammate. This, thought Beers, was applying science to sport.

The other thing he was enthusiastic about was the creation of his new country. He came of age with Canada. Like so many of his fellow citizens, he was caught up in the excitement of uniting the old British colonies. New parliament buildings had risen in the new capital of Ottawa, but his Montreal remained the largest city and the cultural and economic center of the nation.

What better way to blend his interests than to declare lacrosse Canada's national game. It had certainly become all the rage in the Montreal area, and with his help, that passion was spreading. At a convention held in Kingston, Ontario, on September 26, 1867, delegates from twenty-nine clubs formed the Canadian National Lacrosse Association, amended Beers' Rules and adopted a constitution. Within a year, there were eighty Association member clubs.

That confederation year also saw Beers' Rules used in Toronto, where four thousand spectators witnessed the Six Nations' thrilling 3–2 victory over Toronto on the grounds of the Toronto Cricket Club. Toronto soon boasted six hundred players on thirteen new clubs.

In 1868, Montreal merchant T.J. Claxton donated four flagpoles and magnificent banners bearing the Lacrosse Association motto "Our Country, Our Game" for the first national championship. The twelve-club tournament was held at the Brant Lacrosse Club in Paris, Ontario, with Beers officiating all games. St. Regis defeated Prescott 2–0 to win the final.

"If our National Game, while exercising the manly virtues, also trains the national and the moral, it will undoubtedly help to make us better men, and genuine pluck will never go out of fashion in Canada," wrote Beers.

OPPOSITE:

Dr. George Beers — The Father of Lacrosse.
Painting by David Craig

Toronto lacrosse match for the 1873 championship, Montreal vs Toronto.

From a sketch by Wm. Cruikshanks in the *Canadian Illustrated News.*
Library and Archives Canada

"The best players are early risers. No sluggish snoozing after five or six but up while 'silken dalliance in the wardrobe lies' and out in the blue unclouded morning, on a fresh green meadow, where one's blood is set a boil, and put into such healthy circulation that appetites are made ravenous for breakfast."

One pitfall in the game's progress was its association with violence. There were those who would use sport as an opportunity to take out their aggression. That style of play was bound to cause injuries. At one game, an Iroquois chief challenged Beers to keep his Montrealers under control: "You can't play like that. You smash heads, cut hands, make blood. We play all day; no hurt."

One of Beers' Rules stated: "No Indian must play in a match for a white club unless previously agreed upon." The rule was intended to prevent clubs from gaining unfair advantage by bringing in "ringers," superior players who were not members of the competing club. Many Natives had played the game and honed their skills since childhood. Their running ability and stamina were legendary.

Of course, these rules changed lacrosse forever. There was no going back. The game was no longer a contest to settle disputes between villages, nor was it a spiritual game to please the gods, nor would it be used to cure individual or community problems. But the game could never deny its Native origins or its role in Canada's heritage.

George Beers had been but sixteen years old in 1859 when he first proposed lacrosse as his nation's game. In April 1867, four months before the creation of the Dominion of Canada, he published a letter in the *Montreal Daily News* entitled "Lacrosse — our national field game." And in 1869, his book *Lacrosse: The National Game of Canada* appeared, proudly recounting his efforts to establish the game.

For his many contributions to the game, including his rules for standardized play and his tireless efforts to promote the sport in Canada and overseas, William George Beers is known today as "the Father of Modern Lacrosse."

Kahnawake Lacrosse Team with
Dr. George Beers & Henry Beckett, about 1867.
McCord Museum

Kahnawake Lacrosse Club, Quebec, 1867.
McCord Museum

THE Cradle OF LACROSSE

Lacrosse
The Ancient Game

Map illustration by David Craig

Mackinaw City
①

Lake Huron

Lake Michigan

LONDON

Detroit ●

Important Milestones and Locations

1. Fort Michilimackinac – The Great Ruse, 1763
2. Brébeuf and the Hurons, 1637
3. Paris – First Canadian National tournament, 1868
4. Toronto – First game using Beers' Rules, 1867
5. Tyendinaga – Birthplace of the Peacemaker, 1400s or earlier
6. Kingston – First National Lacrosse meeting, 1867
7. George Beers – The Father of Lacrosse, 1860s
8. Montreal – First demonstration by Mohawks, 1834
9. Niagara Falls – Home of the Cayuga Thunder Beings
10. Buffalo – Second U.S. Club, 1868
11. Salamanca – Handsome Lake Vision occurs, 1799
12. Onondaga – Burial place of Handsome Lake, 1815
13. Ogdensburg – First international non-Native game, 1868
14. Saratoga Springs – First lacrosse demonstration in U.S., 1867
15. Cohoes Falls – Peacemaker meets Mohawks, 1400s or earlier
16. Troy – First non-Native club in the U.S., 1867
17. John Flannery – Father of U.S. Lacrosse, 1870s
18. First U.S. university teams, 1877
19. New York – First Nations demonstration by Mohawk & Blackfeet, 1869
20. Baltimore — Lacrosse started by Baltimore A.C., followed by the Druids A.C. & the beginning of Johns Hopkins L.C., 1878–1883

First Nations Communities

A. Six Nations of the Grand River
B. Tyendinaga Mohawk Nation
C. Akwesasne Mohawk Nation
D. Kahnawà:ke Mohawk Nation
E. Tuscarora Nation
F. Allegany Seneca Nation
G. Onondaga Nation
H. Oneida Nation

The Early Days of Lacrosse in the United States

The first recorded game of lacrosse on United States soil took place in Saratoga Springs, New York, on August 7, 1867. It was during the horseracing season, and a "troupe of Indians" — most likely Caughnawaga (Kahnawake) Mohawk — played a demonstration game at the local fairgrounds.

Though this was the first reference made by any newspaper to lacrosse being played in the United States, many young soldiers would have had their first taste of games such as lacrosse and baseball while biding time between battles during the recent Civil War. These veterans had since returned to their communities with the desire to recreate and play — sport serving as a tonic for what they had been through.

A few months later, John L. Flagg, president of the Van Renessalaer Park Driving Association in Troy, New York, invited the existing Six Nations team down from Ontario to showcase the game. Chief Onwanonsyshon (G.M.H. Johnson) introduced the crowd to the basics of lacrosse on October 16, and the following day, eight Six Nations players took on eight local baseball players. The *Troy Daily Times* noted, "Thousands gained admission and several hundred saw the game from the hills to the east." The winner was no surprise, but grassroots enthusiasm for the game itself won the day.

Despite a poor review of the contest by the *Daily Times*, the demonstration was enough to get the ball rolling for the first non-Native club in America. On December 4, 1867, local aficionado Arthur Vinette organized the Mohawk Lacrosse Club. The Troy team commenced practice in May 1868 and toured Canada in July of that year.

An early tour demonstrating the double-stick style of play also took place in 1868, when former Confederate Colonel S.N. Folsom organized Chickasaw and Choctaw teams to play in Cincinnati and other midwestern cities. Most of these players were veterans of the Confederate Army.

The second club to be formed in the U.S. was the Buffalo-based Maple Leaf Club, composed of Canadians living in that city. Captain Fred Lehman held the team's first practices in April 1868, and their first game was played on September 7 against the strong Prescott team from Ontario. This was the first international game played by non-Native teams in the United States.

The Prescott team, along with a team from Caledonia, Ontario, had played in the U.S. on July 4, on an invitation from Ogdensburg, New York. That successful demonstra-

---

Lacrosse Rules in Other Games

Basketball owes many of its rules to lacrosse. Canadian James Naismith, who invented basketball in Springfield, Massachusetts, in 1890 and gave its official rules in 1892, had played lacrosse at McGill University in Montreal in the 1880s and later for the New York Lacrosse Club.

Hockey's official rules were written in the 1870s following a model provided by lacrosse.

tion event led to the organization of two local Ogdensburg clubs, St. Lawrence and Oswegatchie, who played each other for the City Championship on September 9.

The "Big Apple" finally attracted the sport in 1869, when two campaigns were undertaken. Thomas Van Cott brought the Mohawk from St. Regis and the Blackfeet from Quebec to play in Jones Wood, in the upper east end of Manhattan, sometime around September 9. They also scrimmaged across the East River, in Brooklyn's Williamsburg neighborhood, a day or so later.

The second contingent was put together by a Mr. John Sellick and the Prescott Lacrosse Club's captain, J.W. Walsh. They played their games at Brooklyn's Capitoline Grounds and in Jersey City. (The Capitoline Grounds would be demolished in 1880 to make way for the housing project now known as Bedford–Stuyvesant.)

The Father of U.S. Lacrosse

An expatriate Montrealer named John R. Flannery would prove as instrumental in igniting interest in lacrosse in America as George Beers had been in Canada.

Flannery was born in the right place at the right time. The Irish-Canadian entered the world in 1850, in the city that would become the first hotbed of the game for non-Native players and fans.

The New World Irish took to lacrosse in a big way. It was a rough-and-tumble game with similarities to the ancient Gaelic sport of hurling. Of course, those descended from the Emerald Isle knew what it took to compete, in sport and in life. Through the late 1840s and early 1850s, hundreds of thousands of Irish had fled the Great Famine

John R. Flannery and his Shamrocks Lacrosse Team.
Courtesy of the U.S. Lacrosse Foundation

Shamrock Lacrosse Club - World Champs, Montreal October 14, 1871

John R. Flannery, Sr. was the father of American Lacrosse First Player in center row reading left to right

ABOVE: *Emblem of Shamrock Lacrosse Club.*

LEFT: *Shamrock Club lacrosse team,
Champions of the World, composite, 1879.*

McCord Museum

to create new lives for themselves and their families in cities such as New York, Boston, Halifax, Montreal and Toronto.

Flannery grew up in Montreal's Irish community and soon proved to be a natural at lacrosse. By the age of seventeen, he was already being touted as a top player of the game and was *the* top player for the Shamrocks L.C. It must have been something to see him charge a net protected by Montreal L.C. goaltender and lacrosse icon George Beers, seven years his senior. Despite the intense rivalry between the Shamrocks and the Montreal L.C., there must have been a high level of respect between Beers and Flannery.

Flannery and his Shamrocks went on to defeat George Beers' Montreal club for the National Championship in 1871, foreshadowing national domination by the Shamrocks in the late seventies.

But sometime in the mid-1870s, at the height of his playing career, Flannery was faced with a life-altering decision when he was offered work at Standard Oil in Boston, as well as a key role on that city's Union Lacrosse Club. Flannery accepted the invitation and soon packed his bags and sticks and moved south. The move would change not only John Flannery's life, but also the future of lacrosse in North America.

Several universities took notice of the sport, and 1877 became a banner year for U.S. lacrosse when New York University and Manhattan College began their teams. The first university lacrosse game in the U.S. was held in Central Park on November 22. NYU was declared the winner with a 2–0 lead over Manhattan College as darkness closed in. Manhattan played one more game that year, against St. Louis College of New York City.

Perhaps the biggest impact on the club-level game came on July 4, 1878, at the National Championship between Boston's Union Club, led by Flannery, and New York City's Ravenswood L.C., when 40,000 fans crammed the Boston Commons to witness a 3–0 whitewash for Union.

This amazing turnout encouraged the Westchester (New York) Polo Club to run a game at its Athletic Festival in Newport, Rhode Island, the following month. A Baltimore Athletic Club delegation saw the game for the first time there and brought the rules and equipment back to Maryland. Baltimore A.C., Druid A.C. and Johns Hopkins soon started up teams.

Shamrocks L.C. vs New York L.C.,
Championship of America, 1881.
Library and Archives Canada

THE BIRTH OF WOMEN'S LACROSSE

Although the Creator's game fell in the realm of male activities for both the Ongwehonwe Haudenosaunee and the early non-Native clubs, there were eighteenth-century Native precedents for the game being played by women. There is historical mention of mixed games played by the Shawnee and Dakota, and in 1765 it was noted that there were women's games within the Cherokee Nation.

The first recorded non-Native women's match was played at St. Leonard's School in Scotland in 1890. Headmistress Louisa Lumsden and her successor, Frances Dove, had visited North America in 1884 and had seen a game between the Montreal Lacrosse Club and the Caughnawaga (Kahnawake) Mohawk. A few years later, when St. Leonard's required a suitable Spring Term activity for its young ladies, it was decided that a lacrosse program would be just the thing. The team played its first match on March 27, 1890. That same year, an all-girls team was initiated at Princess Helena College, just outside of London.

Lacrosse had crossed the Atlantic from North America to Scotland, but it would have to make the return trip before the women's game would take off in the U.S. Rosabelle Sinclair brought the sport with her from St. Leonard's and established the first women's lacrosse team in America, at the Bryn Mawr School in Baltimore, in 1926. In 1992, Sinclair became the first woman inducted into the National Lacrosse Hall of Fame.

Following their humbling National Championship defeat by Boston's Union Club, Ravenswood enticed Flannery to move to Brooklyn, and he did so in 1879. Flannery would end up spreading enthusiasm for the sport by playing for a total of five clubs in New York: Ravenswood L.C., New York L.C., the Williamsburg Athletic Club, the Brooklyn Athletic Club and the New York Athletic Club.

Flannery organized the National Amateur Lacrosse Association that same year. The NALA started with nine teams in New York City, upstate New York, Boston and Pennsylvania. He also encouraged the growth of the game at universities in New York and New Jersey.

John Flannery had arrived in America at just the right time for lacrosse. He remained in Brooklyn until his death in 1921. Sources say Flannery grew into a talented teacher, organizer, promoter and coach — all attributes that served him well in a life dedicated to the game.

A retired "international trophy" bearing his name is on display at the U.S. Lacrosse Hall of Fame in Baltimore, and a rare few readers of this book may own one of the "Flannery Celebrated Lacrosse Sticks" that he began producing at the end of the 1800s.

John R. Flannery was an intelligent and ambitious player and emissary for his sport, and today is rightly regarded as the "Father of American Lacrosse."

U.S. Lacrosse Goes to School

Intercollegiate lacrosse in the United States began in the Big Apple in 1877, when New York University started its program, with encouragement from New York University Athletic Association president Louis Whitson. Manhattan College also started its lacrosse program around this time. In terms of bragging rights, it remains unclear which school actually started its program first.

On November 22, 1877, the first U.S. intercollegiate lacrosse game was played in Central Park between NYU and Manhattan. St. Louis College of New York City fielded a team to play against Manhattan later that year.

In the spring of 1879, several Harvard students — notably Charles F. Squibb, Sam McDonald and Richard Sturgis — put together a team for their university.

Princeton and Columbia both fielded teams in 1881, with Yale joining the fray the following year. NYU, Harvard, Princeton, Columbia and Yale soon became the big five teams of college lacrosse. At the university level, the sport had never looked stronger, and on March 11, 1882, the Intercollegiate Lacrosse Association was formed.

By 1893, all five of these schools had dropped their lacrosse programs. But four colleges — Cornell, Johns Hopkins, Lehigh and Stevens Institute of Technology — carried the stick forward. Johns Hopkins and Lehigh first fielded teams in 1888. Stevens Tech, of Hoboken, New Jersey, assembled their first team in 1885, a program that continues to this day, making it the longest-running continuous college lacrosse program in the country.

U.S. High School Lacrosse Begins in Brooklyn

While John Flannery did not "invent" high school lacrosse in Brooklyn, New York, his influence was instrumental in establishing it there. And Brooklyn was arguably the first place in the United States where high school lacrosse was played on a sustained level.

Flannery moved to Brooklyn in 1879. During his time in Brooklyn, he played for the Ravenswood LC, then for the New York LC, the Williamsburg AC, the Brooklyn LC and the New York AC. In 1885, he organized and became the first president of the Metropolitan New York Lacrosse Association.

All of this laid the groundwork for the phenomenal success of the Crescent AC, which was based in Brooklyn. They remained one of the best club teams in the United States well into the twentieth century.

Given the popularity of lacrosse in Brooklyn, it soon started to be played in several Brooklyn high schools. In 1916, an interscholastic league was formed. The league was comprised of Manual Training, Erasmus Hall, Boys' High, Jamaica, Flushing, St. John's Prep and Stevens Prep (Hoboken, New Jersey). Poly Prep re-established a team in 1919 after an absence of about ten years. Following Brooklyn's lead, teams were eventually started on Long Island in Nassau and Suffolk counties.

National Lacrosse Hall of Famers Red Gould (Dartmouth), Joe Wilder (Dartmouth), Lou Robbins (Syracuse), Miller Moore (Penn) and Harry Beggs (Yale) all played high school lacrosse in Brooklyn.

In addition, the following All-Americans played high school lacrosse in Brooklyn: Tony Sessa, Ed Schwab, Charlie Wardell and Eddie Green (Princeton); Omar Latimer, Chick Gardiner, Al Edwards, Red Stephens and George Stock (Penn); Dick Hannah and Jack Madden (Yale); and Joe Rooney, Sam Tieman, Al Erda, Sid Roth and Bob Moore (Cornell).

Joe Finn — *Archivist, U.S. Lacrosse*

The Royals See a Lacrosse Match

They say everyone has a high point in their life. For George Beers that great moment came when his favorite sport was played in front of Queen Victoria, the reigning monarch of England and the entire British Empire.

Beers had been part of an exhibition match during Prince Edward's visit to Canada in 1860, but it had always been a dream of his to take his beloved game to England.

In 1867, Her Majesty witnessed lacrosse played by squads brought to England through the efforts of Captain W.B. Johnston, a member of Beers' Montreal Lacrosse Club. Eighteen Caughnawaga (Kahnawake) and Akwesasne Mohawks played at the Crystal Palace, one of the world's premier venues, designed to showcase Britain's leadership and influence. The teams went on to play across the country and appeared at the World's Fair in Paris.

Queen Victoria took pride in bringing British rule of law and good government to her people wherever they may be. They were certainly as diverse as the geographies they inhabited. Perhaps her most interesting subjects were the North American Natives. Romantic tales abounded of these fascinating and exotic people who seemed linked to the dawn of time. While Britain was enthralled with the spread of civilization and with the new inventions and industries that seemed to appear almost daily, North America still held people who roamed free, wild and untouched by progress, at least in the popular imagination. There were many in the crowded and dirty industrial cities who regretted the loss of their own space and freedom, and who saw these "lords of the forest," nature's noblemen, as the people closest to God.

In 1876, Beers organized a second tour of Britain, with both white and Native teams. At the ripe old age of thirty-three, Beers was now a successful dentist and head of Canada's first dental college, but it was through lacrosse that he had touched fame, and he was still competitive as a player and passionate as a promoter of the game.

On June 26, a command performance lacrosse match was held before Queen Victoria. The ceremony and game took place at Windsor Castle, on turf next to the walls of the Italian Garden. High tea was served and the Caughnawaga team performed a ceremonial war dance in full dress.

Mr. J. Lowther, the Under Secretary for the Colonies, presented the players from both teams to the Queen. George Beers gave a short but proud speech, and the Queen responded. Beers was thrilled.

OPPOSITE:

Queen Victoria Sees a Lacrosse Game.
Painting by David Craig

Indian European Team "1883." At Scarborough 25th July.

Lefaivre. Leclaire. White Eagle. "Big John" Patten. Dominique. Dirker. Cpt. Beauvais. Little John. Hemlocks. Strong Arm. Norton. Morice.

*"Big John" and the
Kahnawake lacrosse team,
European competitors,
Scarborough, England, 1883.*
McCord Museum

The most prominent Caughnawaga, Big Jean Baptiste, the team captain, now stood before the Queen dressed in the splendid ceremonial robes of his tribal office. Big John stood six foot two, his athleticism and courage legendary. He was nicknamed "King of the Rapids" because he regularly dared the churning waters of the Lachine Rapids back home in Quebec. His stature and dignity were of the highest order. Here was one proud leader addressing another.

Big Jean knelt, placed his ceremonial tomahawk on the ground before Her Majesty, and presented her with a finely crafted basket. His speech, in the traditional Iroquois language, referred to Queen Victoria as "Our Great and Good Mother." It touched the Queen's heart. Her Majesty gave Big Jean a medal, which he treasured for the rest of his life.

George watched all of this in quiet solemnity, but inside he was beaming with pride. He joined the other players in stepping forward to receive an autographed photograph of the ruler of the Empire.

In the match, the Caughnawaga wore tight-fitting sashes, blue velvet waist belts, scarlet

*Prince Arthur at a lacrosse match,
in Montreal, Quebec, 1869.*
McCord Museum

feathers, and blue caps overlaid with ornamental beadwork. The large "C" on the front may have stood for Caughnawaga or even Canada. In her diary that night, Queen Victoria noted that the white team had fourteen on the field, while the Native side had but thirteen. All in all, she wrote, the game was "very pretty to watch."

When the Queen endorsed something, people took notice and wanted to see it for themselves. George Beers took his lacrosse teams around the British Isles, playing before enthusiastic crowds everywhere they went. In the end, he considered the trip a tremendous success.

Beers returned to Britain in 1883 when the Canadian Department of Agriculture sponsored a large trip featuring Iroquois lacrosse players. The idea was to promote immigration to Canada in order to populate the prairies provinces.

Over 150,000 leaflets were distributed to spectators in several British cities. Sixty games were played from May to July that summer. Thirty-six thousand pounds of a specially prepared *Canadian Illustrated News* supplement were given out.

The game George Beers loved was getting the promotion it rightly deserved.

Canadian and Kahnawake lacrosse teams competing in Europe, 1876.

McCord Museum

International Growth of the Game

◇ Montreal L.C. member J. Weir started a club in Glasgow, Scotland, in 1867.

◇ George Beers promotion of the game led to 29 clubs being formed in Canada in the summer of 1867.

◇ Former Montreal L.C. player Dr. T. Archer formed a lacrosse club from his cross-country club, "The Thames Hare and Hounds," in England in 1875. They practiced on Wimbledon Common. Archer persuaded Beers to make the journey to England in 1876.

◇ The pioneer of lacrosse in Australia was a Canadian named Lambton L. Mount, from Orangeville, Ontario. He had come to Victoria's goldfields with his family in 1853, at the age of 14, but it was not until 1875 that he decided to revive his early boyhood memories of lacrosse. In April 1876 Mount wrote to the *Australasian Newspaper* to announce that he was arranging to import 40 lacrosse

sticks from Canada and intended to establish the Melbourne Lacrosse Club. Fifteen to 20 players took part in the club's first practice match, at Albert Park on June 22, 1876. By 1879, four clubs had been formed, with some 120 players. Melbourne, Fitzroy, South Melbourne and Carlton formed the Victorian Lacrosse Association in July 1879 for the purpose of coordinating matches. The Governor of Victoria, the Most Hon. G.A.C. Phipps, was its inaugural patron.

◇ The game spread to New Zealand in 1878.

◇ Former Beers teammate J.R. Middlemiss took the game to America's west coast in 1878, captaining a team in San Francisco.

◇ Though a great number of Irish immigrants to the U.S. and Canada were playing the game by 1879, this was the year the game found a home in Ireland.

PART III

The Artist of the Game

The Stickmaker

The man squatted at the edge of the cornfield where it met a hardwood forest. He peered into the stand of trees. In the tradition of his ancestors, he tossed small bits of tobacco into the flames of the fire and offered the ancient thanksgiving.

At the end of his prayer, he began his request: "Forest, provided by our Creator — as all of the creatures, plants, earth, air and water are provided by the Creator — I ask for your help. I ask to be guided by our grandfather to a hickory tree, as I am to make a special stick to honor one of our finest *dehuntshigwa'es* players."

"Forest, I thank you for the gifts you provide us — wood and bark to make our homes with, sanctuary for birds and animals that supply our food and clothes, fruits and plants that become our food and medicine — and I honor you and ask your guidance to help me with my desire."

He placed the last of the tobacco in the fire.

The man then stood up, gathered his large hatchet, satchel of tools, rifle, powder and shot, and walked into the lush green woods. He was called Uh Nuh Sah Gun Ga Ge ("Old House"). He wore his hair long, in a ponytail, and his upper body bore several tattoos — clan symbols, lightning and flames. He was an Onondaga, of his mother's Wolf clan. His father, Hagawi'dro'ge' ("Moving Ice"), was of the Turtle clan and had been well respected for his craftsmanship. His father had taught him his art.

He walked further into the woods, crossing several small brooks and rocky outcrops. He passed several small hickory groves scattered among the maple and beech trees, but these were not quite what he was looking for. Finally, he came to a large hill and started up its slope.

It was May and, a moon ago, the Thunder Entities had come through the valley where his people lived. They had played their game in the sky. It had been a rough-and-tumble affair. They had thrown their lightning bolts like hard shots from a player's stick.

Looking back on the creation of this stick, it was as if the wood had spoken to him and told him the right way to shave, bend and cut it.

OPPOSITE:
The Stickmaker.
Painting by David Craig

Minnesota Ojibwe
1823

He thought to himself, "I know the Creator will guide me, because he gave us Sahgone Go Hi Yo Hstah ("He Makes Their Minds Happy"), such a talented player, and I would honor his gift by crafting the best stick out of the best wood I can find. The forest will give me this wood."

Uh Nuh Sah Gun Ga Ge generally preferred to find and cut his wood in November, once the sap had run out of the trees, as there was less breakage while working such wood. But everything comes in its time, and now was the time to make this stick.

He heard a piercing call and looked up the hill to the right, where he saw a large red-tail circling just above the treeline. One of the clans was guiding him. He quickened his pace as he headed toward the raptor.

As he pulled himself up over the last row of boulders and into a small clearing, he saw a majestic mature hickory standing alone. He smiled. It was the height of ten men — much bigger than those he had seen on the way up — and its bark was grey and shaggy. One side of it was charred and black. Fortune had shone on him. The tree had been struck by lightning. The Seven Thunder Entities had aimed their bolts at this lone hickory. Perhaps it had served as one of the goals during their game.

Luckily, it was early in the afternoon. He would have time to cut the tree down and take several eight-foot splits out of it. It was important to select the strongest part of the tree — the smooth, knot-free grain that could be steamed and bent. It was truly the most perfect tree to fashion a lacrosse stick from.

He used the wedges in his satchel to pry the planks into four-inch-wide lengths. He then looked around the site and saw a cache of hickory nuts that must have fallen from a squirrel's nest during the storm. He gathered twenty or so of the hard-shelled seeds and put them in his deerskin satchel. Before leaving the site, he walked in a circle around the tree and examined the ground.

He saw it — a small, flat stone like the ones you find by the lake, worn smooth by the water. His elders had told him that if you keep your eyes open, and you are fortunate, you might find the stone that the Thunder Entities used as their ball. If you find one near a lightning strike, you should keep it, because it will tell you when rain is coming; it will become moist. He picked it up and put it in his satchel with the nuts.

He hung his satchel strap around his neck and balanced the thin planks on his shoulder, steadying them with one arm, then gathered his rifle and hatchet with his free arm. As he made his way back down the hill, he could see the edge of the forest, the cornfield and the homes of his village in the distance — a hawk's-eye view.

On the way home, whenever he found a small clearing he would drop a hickory nut and kick some earth over it. He knew he must replenish whatever he took from the forest. It took a man's lifetime for a hickory tree to grow to at least fourteen inches in diameter, the proper size for stickmaking.

It was early evening when he reached the cornfield. He put his load down and took the tobacco from his satchel. He laid it at the edge of the forest and, using his flint and a piece of dry cedar bark, he started a small fire. He gave thanks to the forest and to the Creator for the gifts that had been given him. The Creator had been generous and he was grateful.

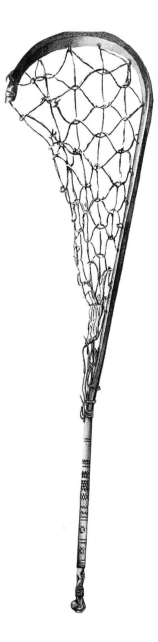

He woke up early the next morning. The central fire that had kept them warm that chilly May night had been reduced to coals. His wife, Ga-ie' to' ("Doing the Same"), would soon be up to feed it and get it going for the first meal of the day. He was careful not to wake his family as he stepped out the front door of his cabin — log homes had gradually replaced the longhouses for which his people were named.

It was a clear day, the sun was just creeping above the eastern horizon and a half moon was still visible in the west. He walked to the edge of the cornfield and faced the rising sun. He began his thanksgiving prayer to the Creator. He thanked the Creator for the continuation of the cycle of life and for all the things that support us. For the air — the air we breathe, the four winds, the birds, the clouds, the sun, the moon and the stars. He thanked Him for all things connected with the land — the plants, the medicine, the animals, the food, friends, family, his people, great teachers and ancestors. He thanked the Creator for all things connected with water — the water we drink, the fish, the plants, turtles, waterfowl, beaver, muskrats and other water animals. A final heartfelt *nya:weh* ("thanks") ended the prayer.

He looked back towards his home. The planks of hickory he had brought back yesterday rested against the log wall. He knew his wife and daughter would not have touched them. They knew the power they carry as women would affect the holistics of the wood. The Creator's game was in the men's realm. He looked forward to starting work on the stick.

Cayuga
pre 1845

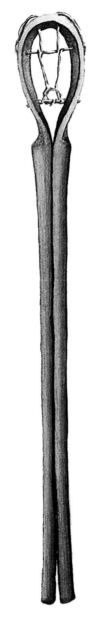

Choctaw
Split-handled Stick

After a breakfast of sagamite and corn biscuits, he brought his tools out to the work area beside the cabin. This included his worktable and a wooden form that he had built to bend the wood once it was steamed and ready for shaping. Sometimes he did the bending between two trees that grew close together, but today he would use the form.

He selected one of the hickory lengths and held it in his hands while he meditated upon it. He began to see the shape of the stick, and the stick saw the player, and so the team began, the player and the stick. He wedged the stave between his legs, the top pointing away from him. His two-handled drawknife was freshly sharpened and ready for use. With both hands, he pulled the knife along the edge between the bark and the wood, shaving the top part of the stick clean.

The drawknife didn't chatter or gouge the stave, so he knew he had picked the right end to work from — with the grain. He finished the rough shaping of this piece of wood and repeated his actions for all six pieces — meditating and envisioning the stick, then carving it out in his mind before beginning the shaving process.

He had started a fire and placed a large pot of water over it to heat. The lid on the pot had a hole in it large enough to receive about half the stick. He threw a few more small logs on the fire and brought the water to a boil. He directed the first split into the opening and left it for a while.

While he waited, he set up the simple wooden form on the table. It was the length of his arm, a flat piece of wood with three separate pieces of wood attached to it. The two outside pieces were in the shape of the crook found at the head of a lacrosse stick. The central piece was more rectangular, and the space between the centerpiece and the outside pieces was just wide enough for the shaft to fit inside.

He pulled the split from the pot and placed it between the middle and end piece of the form. Using all his strength, he put the first bend in the wood. He tied it off with gut so that it would retain its shape. He spent the rest of the morning putting the first bends in the hickory splits that he had shaved down earlier.

After a midday meal of venison, he returned to his worktable. He refreshed the water in the pot and stoked the fire with more logs. He took each of the lengths with the first bend in them and re-steamed them. It was time to put the second bend into each of the shafts. This time, he used the other outside form with the middle piece as his fulcrum.

After the second bend, he tied the sticks off again and put them in a rack beside his cabin, stacking them one atop the other. They would stay there until the end of the summer, when he would begin the final work to ready the stick for the game.

Sahgone Go Hi Yo Hstah thought back on the year so far. Just after the final snowmelt, he had been chosen by the elders to deliver a message to each of the other nations in the Confederacy to the west. As is the ancient protocol, he had created wampum strings. These would signify the authority he had been given and the honesty, sincerity and truth in his words, as he visited each village. Also, it had been decided that a game would be played between two of the clans, Wolf and Turtle. Sahgone Go Hi Yo Hstah was a member of the Wolf clan. You may be a Mohawk, a Cayuga or an Oneida, but if you are a Wolf clan member you are family to all fellow Wolf clan members. The clan is your family regardless of your nation. Not all nations have the same number of clans (for instance, Mohawk have three, Cayuga have five, Onondaga have nine), but all men are related, and especially so through the clan.

Sahgone Go Hi Yo Hstah had less than two weeks to travel through Cayuga, Seneca and Tuscarora lands to spread word of the game and return. Another warrior, Ga Ren Re' ("Steep"), of the Turtle clan, had been chosen to deliver the message to the Oneida and the Mohawk. At each major village, they would stop at the edge of the community and perform the ceremony that allowed them to deliver the message properly. Members of that village would then receive them and take them to their respective chiefs. They would deliver their message from memory while displaying their wampum strings. The wampum strings were to be left with the village, to be returned on the day of the game. At each village, the messengers would stay the evening to receive the hospitality of their clans.

In this way, the news of the late September game between Turtle and Wolf clans was disseminated to the entire Confederacy.

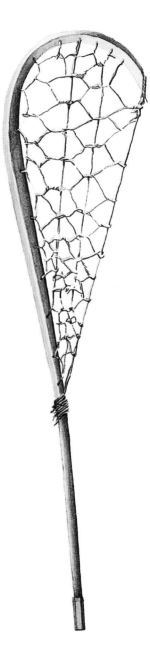

Iroquois 1860

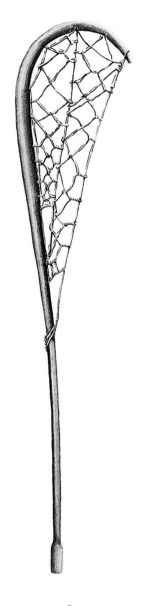

Mohawk
pre 1875

Sahgone Go Hi Yo Hstah had asked Uh Nuh Sah Gun Ga Ge to make him a stick unlike any other. He wanted the Creator to be pleased with how he played in the coming game. This game was special. It was not nation against nation, nor for healing an ill tribe member. It was clan against clan, and it was important for the Confederacy to see the talents of its men and for the clans to show their solidarity.

The British and the French had battled some years ago, and now it looked like the Americans and the British would fight over the same territory. But this time, the fighting would take place on lands belonging to the Ongwehonwe Haudenosaunee. As before, pressure was being put on the individual nations of the Confederacy to commit support to one side or the other. This was not good. This game would celebrate the important clan ties among men — and women — of all Confederacy nations. It would strengthen the unity of the people of the Six Nations.

Sahgone Go Hi Yo Hstah had already begun his training for the game. He ran down deer over miles, tied cloth sandbags to his ankles so that he would feel light when he removed them, and swam against the current in the river for strength. He had also begun a special diet: no rabbit, for it might make you timid during the game; no frog meat, for it might make your bones too brittle for the game's hard physical play. And each day, he meditated, igniting the good mind to create good thoughts, to create a great game.

As game day drew nearer, he would not see women, and he would purge himself using plants provided by the Faithkeeper, Dao Jao Dre ("A Flat Prairie with a Raging Fire Coming Towards You Across the Horizon"). The day before the game, he would join the other players for a special blessing down at the creek, where they would dip their sticks in the water to make them strong and work well. He looked forward to testing the stick Uh Nuh Sah Gun Ga Ge was creating for him.

Soon it was the end of the summer. He felt strong — all his training had made him lean and sinewy. He felt he could run forever. Wolf clan practices had taken on greater meaning as the day of the game advanced toward them. Uh Nuh Sah Gun Ga Ge had told him to come for his stick after the first chill. Last night, he had felt the unseasonable chill of that first evening that declares fall is fast approaching. Tomorrow he would go to the stickmaker's cabin and receive his stick.

It was a beautiful morning. The corn was tall and ready for harvest. Uh Nuh Sah Gun Ga Ge sat at his workbench. He had just finished tying off the final gut string in Sahgone Go Hi Yo Hstah's stick.

All that was left to do was to put his maker's mark on the stick — a large X with marks in the space formed by each angle of the X. He took a sharp piece of flint and made the mark on the back of the handle near the head of the stick. He applied some dye in the cut and wiped away the excess. Looking back on the creation of this stick, it was as if the wood had spoken to him and told him the right way to shave, bend and cut it. The pocket was made from woodchuck hide — the best — and the ball sat perfectly in it.

As Uh Nuh Sah Gun Ga Ge was holding up the stick for final inspection, Sahgone Go Hi Yo Hstah came up from behind him and said with a laugh, "I had to choose between you and my son to make my stick. I hope I chose correctly!"

"I think this stick is the finest one I have ever made," replied Uh Nuh Sah Gun Ga Ge. "Perhaps I should save it for a real ball player!"

The stickmaker handed the stick to the player. "What do you think?"

Sahgone Go Hi Yo Hstah carefully took the stick from Uh Nuh Sah Gun Ga Ge. He held it up and sighted along the handle from the bottom of the stick up to the head, squinting one eye as he scrutinized its line. He flashed the sign of complete approval, a short upward nod of his head and a puckering of his lips. He then placed his hands on the stick as if he were carrying the ball, feeling the weight of it in his hands.

"Do you have a ball?" he asked.

Uh Nuh Sah Gun Ga Ge looked around, then smiled as he reached into his satchel and pulled out the Thunderer's stone. "Here, try this. It is close in weight, even though it is pretty flat." He flipped it to Sahgone Go Hi Yo Hstah, who instinctively snatched the stone out of the air with the stick.

He cradled the ball with both hands on the stick, then with each hand, high and low, spinning his body to protect the "ball" from imaginary opposing warriors. And then, in one motion, he flipped the stone back to Uh Nuh Sah Gun Ga Ge, who caught it just before it hit him.

Creek
pre 1883

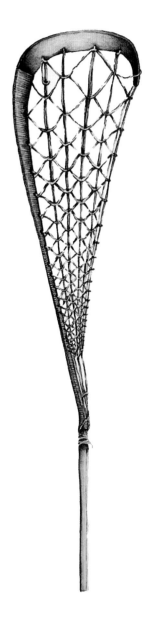

Onondaga
Northern U.S.

"Hey, it's starting to sweat," said Uh Nuh Sah Gun Ga Ge. "Must be a storm coming soon."

Sahgone Go Hi Yo Hstah brought the head of the stick closer toward him and studied the intricate weaving that the stickmaker had undertaken. It was a beautiful stick — finely polished hickory, perfectly balanced — and it looked like it would throw well.

"Nya:weh!" said Sahgone Go Hi Yo Hstah in gratitude.

He reached into his satchel and brought out a parcel and handed it to Uh Nuh Sah Gun Ga Ge. It was tobacco.

"I can see that you have made me a stick that is unlike any other I have ever had. I will play my hardest in the clan game, for the Creator's entertainment."

Sahgone Go Hi Yo Hstah walked back to his cabin, cradling the stick as he went. The stick and the player, a perfect team.

It was the time of the midwinter ceremonies. The snow was deep, the autumn lacrosse game now just a fond memory, a story to pass on to the young. The midwinter ceremonies brought their own activities and celebrations. There had been a snowsnake competition outside of the longhouse. A track of one hundred feet had been built up, a long snow berm three feet off of the ground, with a hollowed-out U-shaped track running its length. The young men had been competing all morning, taking turns with their individual "snakes" — six-to-eight-foot polished sticks with a weighted head carved at one end. The shorter ones, around three feet long, were called "mudcats."

Competitors would run toward the berm with one hand holding the snake parallel to the ground and one finger of the other hand positioned at the back end of the stave. It took great skill to launch the snake into the U-track and have it travel the length of the course. You had to take all of your power and concentrate it into your index finger. Opponents yelled at the tops of their lungs and ran toward the track in attempt to distract the thrower. A great cheer was heard each time there was a successful throw.

Inside the longhouse, preparations were being made for another game. It was the Great Peachbowl Game. This game had been played at annual ceremonies since

Ballplay of the Dakota on the St. Peters River in Winter, Seth Eastman (1808–1875). Oil on canvas, 1848.
Amon Carter Museum of American Art, Fort Worth, Texas

Seminole
Southern U.S.

the Creator and the Uncle played it at the beginning of the world. It would be clan against clan, and everyone in the clan would take their turn, no matter how old or young or your state of physical wellness — if you needed help, the clan, your family, would help you.

The Faithkeepers for each clan were collecting the bets. Dao Jao Dre, the faithkeeper of the Wolf clan, made his way along his people, gathering their bets. Eventually, he came to Sahgone Go Hi Yo Hstah.

"What do you have, Sahgone Go Hi Yo Hstah?"

Sahgone Go Hi Yo Hstah unwrapped the beautiful wooden stick. Even from the back of the dwelling, Uh Nuh Sah Gun Ga Ge could see that Sahgone Go Hi Yo Hstah had added special carvings that were meaningful to him and that told his story. Sahgone Go Hi Yo Hstah handed the stick to the Faithkeeper and moved to the back of the longhouse.

"I saw what you bet," said Uh Nuh Sah Gun Ga Ge. "That must have been hard!"

Sahgone Go Hi Yo Hstah looked at him and replied, "You know the way things go. If I win, I will keep it and one day it will be buried with me so that I can play in the Skyworld. And if I lose, it goes before me to that land, and it will be waiting for me when I take the faceoff. No, my friend, it is not so hard."

The Great Peach Bowl Game commenced. Cheers came from the side that was maneuvering the bowl and making the pits jump and settle. "SHA,SHA,SHA!" chanted the other side as they tried to influence the outcome with the power of one community mind. The tension was thick, but Sahgone Go Hi Yo Hstah felt good.

Win or lose, he would have his stick when he played with his ancestors at the end of his journey on the Skyroad. When that time came, he would run to meet them.

The Fourth Quarter

No. 24.
BALL-PLAY DANCE.
(From Catlin's N.A. Indian Collection)

Ball Play Dance, George Catlin (1796–1872). Lithograph with applied watercolor, 1875–1878.
Amon Carter Museum of American Art, Fort Worth, Texas

Selected Bibliography

Books

Beers, William George. *Lacrosse: The National Game of Canada*. Montreal: Dawson Brothers, 1869.

Fisher, Donald M. *Lacrosse: A History of the Game*. Baltimore: The Johns Hopkins University Press, 2002.

Henry, Alexander. *Travels and Adventures in Canada and the Indian Territories Between the Years 1760 and 1776*. New York: I. Riley, 1809.

Mangan, J.A., ed. *The Cultural Bond: Sport, Empire and Society*. London: Frank Cass & Co. Ltd., 1992.

Morgan, Lewis Henry. *The League of the Ho-de-no-sau-nee or Iroquois*. Rochester, NY: 1851; New York: Cornith Books, reprint 1962.

Morrow, Don. "Lacrosse as a National Game." *A Concise History of Sport in Canada*. Toronto: Oxford University Press, 1989.

North American Indian Travelling College, eds. *Tewaarathon (Lacrosse) — Awkwesasne's Story of Our National Game*. Awkwesasne–St. Regis, 1978.

Thwaites, R.G., ed. *The Jesuit Relations and Allied Documents, Travels and Explorations of the Jesuit Missionaries in New France 1610–1791*. Cleveland: The Burrows Brothers Co., 1898.

Vennum, Thomas. *American Indian Lacrosse: Little Brother of War*. Washington, DC: Smithsonian Institution Press, Washington, 1994.

Vennum, Thomas. *Lacrosse Legends of the First Americans*. Baltimore: The Johns Hopkins University Press, 2007.

Weyand, Alexander M., and Milton R. Roberts. *The Lacrosse Story*. Baltimore: H. and A. Herman, 1965.

Magazine and Journal Articles

Adamski, Barbara K. "An Upstream Battle." *The Walrus.* May 2007.

Fritz, Donald T. "Planting Seeds." *Lacrosse Magazine.* March 1991.

Humber, William. "The Spirit of the Black Bear." *The Idler.* No. 24, July/August 1989.

McPhee, John. "Spin Right and Shoot Left." *The New Yorker.* March 23, 2009.

Poulter, Gillian. "Snowshoeing and Lacrosse: Canada's Nineteenth Century 'National Games.'"
   Sport in Society: Cultures, Commerce, Media, Politics, Volume 6, Issues 2 & 3, 2003.

Rock, Tom. "More Than a Game." *Lacrosse Magazine.* November/December 2002.

Academic Papers

Downey, Allan. "The Creator's Game: A History of Six Nation's Lacrosse 1840s–1990s." Master of Arts
   degree project, Tri-University/Wilfred Laurier University, 2008.

Morrow, Don. "The Canadian Image Abroad: The Great Lacrosse Tours of 1876 and 1883."
   Proceedings of the Fifth Canadian Symposium on the History of Sport and Physical Education.
   Toronto, August 26–29, 1982.

Websites

Aveni, Anthony. "The Indian Origins of Lacrosse." www.history.org.

Dictionary of Canadian Biography, Last modified June 27, 2008. www.biographi.ca.

Price, S.L. "Pride of a Nation." SI Vault, July 19, 2010. http://sportsillustrated.cnn.com/vault/article/
   magazine/MAG1172077/index.htm

Photographs, Paintings and Illustrations

Amon Carter Museum

Canadian Museum of Civilization

Gilcrease Museum

Library & Archives Canada

McCord Museum of Canadian History

Notman Photographic Archives

List of Illustrations

Artist Websites

David Craig:
davidcraigart.com

Arnold Jacobs:
twoturtlenativeart.com

Brian Larney:
yahvlane.com

Lacrosse and Six Nations Museums

- akwesasneculturalcenter.org/museum (Akwesasne Cultural Center)

- canadianlacrossehalloffame.com (Canadian Lacrosse Hall of Fame)

- iroquoismuseum.org (Iroquois Museum)

- museum.oneidanation.org (Oneida Nation Museum)

- olhof.ca (Ontario Lacrosse Hall of Fame)

- senecamuseum.org (Seneca Museum)

- sixnationsindianmuseum.com (Six Nations Indian Museum)

- tuscaroranationnc.com/tuscarora_museum (Tuscarora Nation Museum)

- uslacrosse.org/museum (US Lacrosse Foundation)

- woodland-centre.on.ca (Woodland Cultural Centre Museum)

Acknowledgements

I would like to thank the following people for their participation in the *Lacrosse — The Ancient Game* Project.

First, I must thank our team, who worked so diligently on all aspects of the book: Ron Fletcher, my co-writer, for his unique interpretations of historical data within the European Influence section; Delmor Jacobs (Cayuga, Six Nations), for sharing without hesitation the very special stories of his people with us and overseeing content from a First Nations viewpoint; Gillian Stead, for her wonderful design work and for making all the pieces fit so beautifully; Noel Hudson, for his editing and proofreading expertise; David Craig, for his world-class illustrations of historical moments within the European section; Arnold Jacobs (Onondaga, Six Nations), for his beautiful interpretations of key Iroquois creation stories; and Choctaw artist Brian Larney, for granting permission to borrow from his beautiful painting *American Indian Stickball Collection*. Thanks also to John Denison for his timely advice regarding all things publishing. A special thank you to one of the greatest lacrosse players of all time, Gary Gait, for his foreword, and other wonderful players, Brent Bucktooth, Paul Rabil and Jim Veltman.

Thank you to the Canadian Lacrosse Foundation, the Ontario Lacrosse Association, the US Lacrosse Foundation and the United States Intercollegiate Lacrosse Association for their support.

I want to thank the people at the Museum of Civilization (Ottawa, Ontario) for welcoming Ron and me into the archives, where we held true lacrosse treasures in our hands. Thank you, as well, to the Ontario Lacrosse Hall of Fame.

I want to thank lacrosse historians Stan Shillington (British Columbia Lacrosse), Joe Finn (U.S. Lacrosse), and professors Anthony Aventi of Colgate University and Don Morrow of the University of Western Ontario. Thanks also to Faithkeeper Oren Lyons (Onondaga) and traditional stickmaker Alf Jacques (Onondaga) for conversations on the cultural and historical aspects of the game. Thank you to Grant Jarvis for being a great sounding board and also to his daughter Emma for her research in Ottawa. Thank you to Angela Ryan, Sylvia Barker and Paul Connelly for reading and commenting on parts of the book.

This book would not have been possible without the financial and inspirational support of the following people:

Robert P. Bradley — Kingswood School (West Hartford, Connecticut); Hobart College (Geneva, New York); Toronto Lacrosse Club; Thunderbird Lacrosse (Arizona); Aspen Lacrosse (Colorado); Connecticut Valley Lacrosse Club (Simsbury, Connecticut).

Tom Calder — Baldwin High School (Long Island, New York); Freeport Summer League (New York); Nassau Community College (New York); Hofstra University (New York); Roanoke College (Virginia); Roanoke Summer League; Chapel Hill L.C. (North Carolina); University of North Carolina; Johns Hopkins University.

Paul Connelly — Toronto Lacrosse Club and Birchmount Park Collegiate Institute (Scarborough, Ontario).

Joe Corcoran — Corning East High School (New York); Hobart College; Miller Lacrosse Team (New York); Denver Lacrosse Club; Dallas Lacrosse Club.

Doug Deschner — Burnaby Jr. A (British Columbia); New Westminster Salmonbellies Sr. A (British Columbia); Brooklin Redmen (Ontario); University of Baltimore; Towson Lacrosse Club (Maryland); club teams in Alberta, British Columbia, Manitoba and Ontario; Oshawa Blue Knights (Ontario); Team Alberta; Team Manitoba; Team Canada.

Ward Doonan — Berkshire School (Massachusetts); Seneca Lacrosse Club (New Jersey); Hobart College (New York).

Joe Fusco — Berkshire School (Massachusetts); Seneca Lacrosse Club (New York); Hobart College (New York).

John Griffin — Baldwin High School (Long Island, New York), Freeport Summer League (New York), Cornell University; New Jersey Lacrosse Club; Team USA.

Grant Jarvis — York Mills Titans (Ontario); Toronto Lacrosse Club; Birchmount Park Collegiate Institute (Scarborough, Ontario).

Paddy and Cheryl Mallen — Windsor Minor Lacrosse (Ontario); Windsor Warlocks Jr. B and Senior Lacrosse (Ontario); Toronto Lacrosse Club.

Howie Mulcahey — Hobart College (New York); Houston Lacrosse Club; Honeoye Falls–Lima Youth and Varsity Lacrosse (New York).

Tim Nuland and Kitsy Snow — Hobart College (New York); Wheaton College (Illinois), Manhasset Minor Lacrosse (New York); Orange County Lacrosse Club (California).

Dr. Bob Teasdall — St. Paul's School (Maryland); Johns Hopkins University (Maryland); Toronto Lacrosse Club; Team Canada.

Jayne Traina — my sister, and her late husband, Sal, a brother of mine (Walden, New York).

Delmor Jacobs wanted to make sure I remembered Six Nations historian Rick Hill, who we sat with early on, and his personal mentor, teacher and friend Martin (Marty) Smith.

From a very personal point of view, I must recognize my various lacrosse homes over the years: Baldwin High School; Freeport Summer League; Hobart College; Central Connecticut Valley

Lacrosse Club; University of Massachusetts; Orange County Lacrosse Club (1 game); Malvern Lacrosse Club (Melbourne, Australia); Toronto Lacrosse Club; Toronto Stars Lacrosse Girls Box and Field Program; Birchmount Park Collegiate Boys and Girls Field Programs; Ontario Women's Lacrosse; Team Ontario and Team Canada.

Hobart College was instrumental in developing my personal love of the game. Thank you to the late Jerry Schmidt, Dave Urich, Tom Korn, William Van Arsdale, the late Bill Stiles and Mike Hanna — just some of the many "Statesmen" who loved lacrosse and passed it on.

While at Hobart College and with Team Canada, I played with some of the greatest players in the game and I'll always be thankful for that opportunity.

I want to thank my other family — the rest of the Turks — for being good, supportive friends. You know who you are!

Thank you to Dan Griffin for getting me into sports.

I want to encourage my nephews, Jake and Jack, and my nieces, Alex and Midori, who have taken up the game.

And my special thanks to my wife, Heidi, and my two lacrosse-playing daughters, Geneva and Ella, who have supported my love of the game and my pursuit in producing this book. They have come to love the game, as well.

The Lacrosse Player

by Jim Calder

When he's asked, "What's your sport?"
A crisp ..."Lacrosse!".... is his retort
"Why play such a rough, demanding game?
Is it for money or maybe for fame?"

He replies, "Sure isn't for cash
Cold day in hell when I get paid to slash
And as for the fame bit you've just offered
Fame wouldn't match the injuries I've suffered!"

"No my friend, I play for the love
The feeling I get when I don helmet and glove
The swing of the stick and the snap of the net
Just some of the rewards that I will get"

"And it's the people I know from Miami to Hornpayne
That are picking up the Creator's game
It's the games in the mud, the games in the sun
Simply to compete, whether you've lost or have won."

"The pipe shot that bounces a wee bit wide
The frustrated feeling you get deep down inside
To come back from a lopsided score at the half
Then to win by one so you have the last laugh."

"And it's the people I know from Prince George to Tulane
That are starting to play the Creator's game
And if those aren't enough reasons for me to play
I have a thousand more if you have all day"

"It's the freedom and the people that make it so pure
Because of these qualities the game will endure
Long after we've put away our sticks
Our children's children will be taking their licks"

"Have I answered your question?", the lacrosse player asks
Anxious to return to his favourite game's tasks
For he plays for the entertainment of the Creator above
And for the thrill of competing in the game we all love.

So he turns, and trots back on to the pitch
To play the game that won't make him rich
But value and worth are different than gold
This fact, to me, a lacrosse player once told

This game never ends, in the Sky World we'll play
Try to put a value on that at the end of the day
I will bring my stick and you should bring one along
And we'll play again soon if I'm not half wrong.